United States Government Accountability Office

Report to Congressional Requesters

I0455451

November 2013

GOVERNMENT SUPPORT FOR BANK HOLDING COMPANIES

Statutory Changes to Limit Future Support Are Not Yet Fully Implemented

GAO-14-18

GOVERNMENT SUPPORT FOR BANK HOLDING COMPANIES

Statutory Changes to Limit Future Support Are Not Yet Fully Implemented

GAO Highlights

Highlights of GAO-14-18, a report to congressional requesters

Why GAO Did This Study

The federal government extended unprecedented support to financial institutions to stabilize financial markets during the financial crisis. While these actions helped to avert a more severe crisis, they raised questions about the appropriate scope of government safety nets for financial institutions. GAO was asked to review the benefits that large bank holding companies (those with more than $500 billion in assets) have received from actual and implied government support.

This is the first of two reports GAO will issue on this topic. This report examines (1) actual government support for banks and bank holding companies during the financial crisis, and (2) recent statutory and regulatory changes related to government support for banks and bank holding companies. GAO reviewed relevant statutes, regulations, and agency documents; analyzed program transaction data; and interviewed regulators, representatives of financial institutions, and academics. In a second report to be issued in 2014, GAO will examine any funding or other economic advantages the largest bank holding companies have received as a result of implied government support.

What GAO Recommends

GAO recommends that the Federal Reserve Board establish timeframes for completing its process for drafting procedures related to its emergency lending authority to ensure timely compliance with Dodd-Frank Act requirements. The Federal Reserve Board accepted this recommendation.

View GAO-14-18. For more information, contact Lawrance Evans, Jr. at (202) 512-4802 or EvansL@gao.gov.

What GAO Found

During the 2007-09 financial crisis, the federal government's actions to stabilize the financial system provided funding support and other benefits to bank holding companies and their subsidiaries. Agencies introduced new programs with broad-based eligibility that provided funding support to eligible institutions, which included entities that were part of a bank holding company and others. Programs that provided the most significant support directly to bank holding companies or their subsidiaries included Department of the Treasury capital investment programs, Federal Reserve System lending programs, and Federal Deposit Insurance Corporation (FDIC) guarantee programs. Together these actions helped to stabilize financial conditions, while participating firms also accrued benefits specific to their own institutions, such as liquidity benefits from programs that allowed them to borrow at longer maturities and at interest rates that were below possible market alternatives. At the end of 2008, program use—measured for each institution as the percentage of total assets supported by the programs—was higher on average for banks and bank holding companies with $50 billion or more in total assets than for smaller firms. The six largest bank holding companies were significant participants in several emergency programs but exited most by the end of 2009. Differences in program use were driven in part by how institutions funded themselves. For example, while smaller banks relied more on deposit funding, larger bank holding companies relied more on short-term funding markets and participated more in programs that assisted these markets. In addition to these programs, the Board of Governors of the Federal Reserve System (Federal Reserve Board) granted several regulatory exemptions to allow banks to provide liquidity support to their nonbank affiliates and for other purposes. Finally, government assistance to individual troubled firms benefited these firms, their counterparties, and the financial system.

The Dodd-Frank Wall Street Reform and Consumer Protection Act (Dodd-Frank Act) contains provisions that aim to modify the scope of federal safety nets, restrict future government support and strengthen regulatory oversight for the banking sector, but implementation is incomplete and the effectiveness of some provisions remains uncertain. Agencies have finalized certain changes to traditional safety nets for insured banks, but impacts of provisions to limit the scope of transactions that benefit from these safety nets will depend on how they are implemented. The act also places restrictions on emergency authorities used by regulators during the crisis to assist financial firms. For example, it prohibits the use of these authorities to rescue a specific failing firm. The Federal Reserve Board is required by the act to establish policies and procedures implementing changes to its emergency authority under Section 13(3) of the Federal Reserve Act, but it has not completed its process for drafting the required procedures or set time frames for doing so. Setting time frames could help ensure more timely completion of these procedures. FDIC has made progress toward implementing its new authority under the Dodd-Frank Act to resolve a large failing firm. FDIC continues to work to address potential obstacles to the viability of its resolution process as an alternative to bankruptcy, such as challenges that could arise when resolving more than one failing firm. Finally, the Federal Reserve Board has finalized certain enhanced prudential standards for the largest financial firms intended to reduce the risks these firms could pose to the financial system.

_____ **United States Government Accountability Office**

Contents

Tables

Figures

Abbreviations

ABCP	asset-backed commercial paper
ABS	asset-backed securities
AMLF	Asset-Backed Commercial Paper Money Market Mutual Fund Liquidity Facility
BEA	Bureau of Economic Analysis
CBO	Congressional Budget Office
CDCI	Community Development Capital Initiative
CDS	credit default swaps
COP	Congressional Oversight Panel
CPFF	Commercial Paper Funding Facility
CPP	Capital Purchase Program
DGP	Debt Guarantee Program
EESA	Emergency Economic Stabilization Act of 2008
FDIC	Federal Deposit Insurance Corporation
FHLB	Federal Home Loan Bank
FOMC	Federal Open Market Committee
FRBNY	Federal Reserve Bank of New York
FSOC	Financial Stability Oversight Council
GSE	government-sponsored enterprise
IDI	insured depository institution
ILC	industrial loan corporation
LIBOR	London Interbank Offered Rate
MBS	mortgage-backed securities
MMMF	money market mutual fund
NIC	National Information Center
OCC	Office of the Comptroller of the Currency

OIS	overnight indexed swap
OLA	Orderly Liquidation Authority
PDCF	Primary Dealer Credit Facility
SPOE	Single Point-of-Entry
TAF	Term Auction Facility
TAGP	Transaction Account Guarantee Program
TALF	Term Asset-Backed Securities Loan Facility
TARP	Troubled Asset Relief Program
TIP	Targeted Investment Program
TLGP	Temporary Liquidity Guarantee Program
TSLF	Term Securities lending Facility

GAO

U.S. GOVERNMENT ACCOUNTABILITY OFFICE

441 G St. N.W.
Washington, DC 20548

November 14, 2013

The Honorable Sherrod Brown
Chairman
Financial Institutions and Consumer Protection Subcommittee
Committee on Banking, Housing, and Urban Affairs
United States Senate

The Honorable David Vitter
United States Senate

During the financial crisis of 2007-2009, the federal government extended unprecedented amounts of assistance to financial institutions to stabilize financial markets and the broader economy. This support included the creation of temporary programs that extended more than $1 trillion in loans, provided hundreds of billions of dollars of capital, and guaranteed hundreds of billions of dollars of other liabilities for participating financial institutions. On a few occasions, the federal government provided additional capital and other support to individual large troubled institutions to prevent a bankruptcy that could have further destabilized markets. While these government interventions helped to avert a more severe crisis, they raised questions about moral hazard and the appropriate scope of government safety nets for financial institutions.[1] In particular, extraordinary support for troubled financial institutions led to debate about how to decrease the likelihood of future rescues of failing institutions and limit the potential for federal safety nets intended for insured depository institutions to provide a backstop for activities conducted outside these institutions.

The Dodd-Frank Wall Street Reform and Consumer Protection Act (Dodd-Frank Act) includes provisions intended to prevent government rescues of individual financial institutions, place new restrictions on emergency authorities used by regulators to assist financial institutions during the last financial crisis, and subject a designated group of large financial institutions to stricter regulatory oversight, among other changes.[2]

---

[1]Moral hazard can occur when market participants expect similar emergency actions in future crises, thereby weakening their incentives to properly manage risks.

[2]Pub. L. No. 111-203, 124 Stat. 1376 (2010).

Nevertheless, market observers have continued to debate whether some of the largest and most complex financial institutions—including bank holding companies with more than $500 billion in total consolidated assets—may continue to benefit from expectations of extraordinary government support that could potentially give them funding and other economic advantages relative to smaller competitors.

You asked us to review the economic benefits that the largest bank holding companies (those with more than $500 billion in total consolidated assets) have received as a result of actual or perceived government support. This is the first of two reports we will issue on this topic. In this report, we review (1) support banks and bank holding companies received as a result of government efforts to stabilize financial markets during the financial crisis of 2007-2009, and (2) recent statutory and regulatory changes related to government support for banks and bank holding companies and factors that could impact the effectiveness of these changes. In terms of scope, the first section of this report addresses benefits that bank holding companies and their subsidiaries received *during the crisis* from *actual* government support provided through emergency actions taken. It does not address benefits that some institutions may have received and may continue to receive from *perceived* government support—that is, support that market participants may expect the federal government to provide to these institutions in the event that they face large losses that threaten them with failure. In a second report to be issued in 2014, we will address questions about whether the largest bank holding companies have received funding or other economic advantages as a result of expectations that the government would not allow them to fail. That report will include the results of our original empirical analysis of funding costs for large bank holding companies.

To address the objectives for this report, we reviewed relevant statutes, regulations, agency documents and data, related studies, and prior GAO work. To describe government actions that extended support for banks and bank holding companies during the crisis, we included information and analyses from prior GAO work on the Troubled Asset Relief Program (TARP), the emergency programs of the Board of Governors of the Federal Reserve System (Federal Reserve Board), and other emergency assistance provided to the banking sector. To obtain perspectives on the benefits that bank holding companies and their subsidiaries received from emergency government actions, we reviewed papers by staff of financial regulators and other experts and interviewed federal financial regulators, representatives of bank holding companies that received emergency government assistance, trade associations, and academics. To describe the amount of funding support that institutions of various sizes received from emergency government programs, we obtained and analyzed program transaction data for the programs introduced by the Department of the Treasury (Treasury), the Federal Reserve Board, and the Federal Deposit Insurance Corporation (FDIC) that provided the most significant funding support directly to bank holding companies or their subsidiaries. For selected programs, we compared the terms of this assistance (such as interest rates and fees) to indicators of pricing for market alternatives that might have been available to program participants. While this analysis provides a measure of program pricing versus potential market alternatives, it does not produce a precise quantification of the benefits that accrued to participating financial institutions. To compare the extent to which banking organizations of various sizes used these emergency programs, we calculated the percentage of banking organization assets that were supported by emergency programs—either through capital injections, loans, or guarantees—at quarter-end dates for 2008 through 2012. Finally, we obtained and analyzed Federal Reserve Board documentation of Federal Reserve Board decisions to grant exemptions to Section 23A of the Federal Reserve Act and approve applications from financial companies to convert to bank holding company status.[3]

Our scope did not include an analysis of any benefits that banks or bank holding companies may have received from any expectations of future government support. As discussed earlier, we will cover any benefits to banking entities from perceived government support in our second report. For parts of our work that involved the analysis of computer-processed data, such as transaction data for the agencies' emergency programs, we assessed the reliability of these data and determined that they were sufficiently reliable for our purposes. Appendix I contains additional information about the data sources used and our assessment of the reliability of these data. Appendices III and IV contain additional information about our methodology for the data analyses in our first objective.

To address our second objective, we reviewed information on statutory and regulatory changes related to the authority to provide government support for banks and bank holding companies, including prior GAO work

---

[3]Pub. L. No. 63-43, § 23A, 38 Stat. 251, 272 (1913) (12 U.S.C. § 371c).

on implementation of the Dodd-Frank Act. To update the status of agencies' efforts to implement these changes, we reviewed agencies' proposed and final rules, and interviewed staff from FDIC, the Federal Reserve Board, the Office of the Comptroller of the Currency (OCC), and Treasury. We identified statutory provisions or requirements that agencies had not fully implemented and interviewed agency staff about planned steps to complete implementation. We also reviewed relevant congressional testimonies and other public statements by agency officials. To describe factors that could impact the effectiveness of these provisions, we reviewed prior GAO work on the potential impacts of Dodd-Frank Act provisions. To obtain additional perspectives on factors that could impact the effectiveness of these provisions, we interviewed and reviewed the public statements and analyses of agency officials, academics, and market experts. Appendix I contains additional information on our scope and methodology.

We conducted this performance audit from January 2013 through November 2013 in accordance with generally accepted government auditing standards. Those standards require that we plan and perform the audit to obtain sufficient, appropriate evidence to provide a reasonable basis for our findings and conclusions based on our audit objectives. We believe that the evidence obtained provides a reasonable basis for our findings and conclusions based on our audit objectives.

Background

Bank Holding Companies

Bank holding companies are companies that own or control one or more banks. In the United States, most banks insured by FDIC are owned or controlled by a bank holding company. In addition to bank subsidiaries engaged in traditional banking activities of deposit-taking and lending, many U.S. bank holding companies also own or control nonbank subsidiaries, such as broker-dealers and insurance companies. The Bank Holding Company Act of 1956, as amended, establishes the legal framework under which bank holding companies operate and establishes their supervision, with the Federal Reserve Board having authority over bank holding companies and their banking and nonbanking interests.[4]

---

[4]Pub. L. No. 84-511, 70 Stat. 133 (codified at 12 U.S.C. §§ 1841-1852).

The Bank Holding Company Act also limits the types of activities that bank holding companies may conduct, either directly or through their nonbank affiliates. The restrictions, which are designed to maintain the general separation of banking and commerce in the United States, allow bank holding companies to engage only in banking activities and those activities that the Federal Reserve Board has determined to be "closely related to banking," such as extending credit, servicing loans, and performing appraisals of real estate and tangible and intangible personal property, including securities.[5] Under amendments to the Bank Holding Company Act made by the Gramm-Leach-Bliley Act, also known as the Financial Services Modernization Act of 1999, a bank holding company can elect to become a financial holding company that can engage in a broader range of activities that are financial in nature.[6] The Gramm-Leach-Bliley Act defined a set of activities as financial in nature and authorized the Federal Reserve Board, with the agreement of Treasury, to determine whether an additional activity is financial in nature or incidental or complementary to a financial activity.[7] For example, financial holding companies are permitted to engage in securities underwriting and dealing, but would be prohibited, for example, from selling commercial products. Large U.S. bank holding companies typically are registered as financial holding companies and own a number of domestic bank subsidiaries, as well as nonbank and foreign subsidiaries.

The largest U.S. bank holding companies have grown substantially in size and scope in recent decades. Since 1990, in part due to waves of mergers, the share of total bank holding company assets controlled by the largest 10 firms increased from less than 30 percent to more than 60

---

[5]§ 4(c)(6), 70 Stat. at 137 (codified at 12 U.S.C. § 1843(k)(4)(F)).

[6]Pub. L. No. 106-102, 113 Stat. 1338 (1999) (codified in scattered sections of 12, 15 U.S.C). In order to be a financial holding company: (1) all depository institutions controlled by the bank holding company must be and remain well capitalized; (2) all depository institutions controlled by the bank holding company must be and remain well managed; and (3) the bank holding company must have made an effective election to become a financial holding company. 12 C.F.R. § 225.81(b).

[7]§ 103(a), 113 Stat. at 1342 (codified at 12 U.S.C. § 1843(k)). The financial holding company can engage in activities that the Federal Reserve Board determines (1) are financial in nature or incidental to such financial activity, or (2) are complementary to a financial activity and do not pose a substantial risk to the safety and soundness of depository institutions or the financial system generally. *Id.*

percent, as of July 2012.[8] Some bank holding companies grew to become large financial conglomerates that offer a wide range of products that cut across the traditional financial sectors of banking, securities, and insurance. Following the enactment of the Gramm-Leach-Bliley Act in 1999, the assets held in nonbank subsidiaries or at the holding company level grew to account for a progressively larger share of total bank holding company assets. Greater involvement by bank holding companies in nontraditional banking businesses has been accompanied by an increase in the proportion of bank holding company income that is generated by fee income, trading, and other noninterest activities. As large bank holding companies have broadened the scope of their activities and their geographic reach, they have become more organizationally complex. A simple indicator of organizational complexity is the number of separate legal entities within the bank holding company; the largest four U.S. bank holding companies each had at least 2,000 as of June 30, 2013.[9]

The 2007-2009 financial crisis raised concerns that some U.S. bank holding companies—as well as some nonbank financial institutions—had grown so large, interconnected, and leveraged that their failure could threaten the stability of the U.S. financial system and the global economy. The Dodd-Frank Act includes several provisions intended to reduce the risk of a failure of a large, complex financial institution, the damage that such a failure could do to the economy, and the likelihood that a failing institution would receive government support. For example, the act directs the Federal Reserve Board to impose enhanced prudential standards and oversight on bank holding companies with $50 billion or more in total consolidated assets and nonbank financial companies designated by the

---

[8]An important factor contributing to merger activity was a statutory change removing barriers to geographic expansion by banks. The Riegle-Neal Interstate Banking and Branching Efficiency Act of 1994 authorized interstate mergers between adequately capitalized and managed banks starting in June 1997, regardless of whether the transaction would be prohibited by state law, though states had the right to opt out of that arrangement if they passed legislation prior to June 1997 prohibiting merger transactions with out-of-state banks. Pub. L. No. 103-328, 108 Stat. 2338 (codified at scattered sections of 12 U.S.C.). Previously, most banks that wanted to operate across state lines had to establish a bank holding company and, with certain restrictions, acquire or charter a bank in each state in which they wanted to operate. With the advent of interstate branching, banks that previously were not permitted to expand across state lines could do so by acquiring existing banks, and some multistate bank holding companies could consolidate their operations into a single bank with multistate branches.

[9]One limitation of this indicator is that some legal entities may be vehicles for tax purposes and therefore may not result in a significant increase in organizational complexity.

Financial Stability Oversight Council (FSOC) for supervision by the Federal Reserve Board.[10]

Federal Safety Net Programs for the Banking Sector

The federal government maintains programs—frequently referred to as safety nets—to reduce the vulnerability of depository institutions to runs that could threaten the health of the banking system and the broader economy.[11] Following a series of banking crises in the early 1900s, the government created two programs generally considered to form the core of these safety nets: the Federal Reserve System's discount window and FDIC deposit insurance. By making emergency liquidity available to solvent depository institutions through the discount window and reducing incentives for depositors to withdraw their funds, these safety nets were intended to help ensure that depository institutions could continue to lend and provide other important services, even during turbulent economic conditions. In addition to the discount window and deposit insurance, the Federal Reserve Board and FDIC have other emergency authorities related to maintaining financial stability. Moreover, the Federal Home Loan Bank System serves to provide liquidity to the banking system that helps to foster stability. In part because access to federal safety nets potentially reduced incentives for insured depositors to monitor and restrain the risk-taking of banks, banks were also subjected to federal supervision and regulation.

Discount Window

The Federal Reserve System, in its role as the lender of last resort, operates discount window programs, which provide a backup source of liquidity through collateralized loans for depository institutions to help ensure the stable flow of credit to households and businesses.[12] During normal market conditions, banks and other depository institutions in generally sound financial condition can obtain discount window loans to address short-term funding needs arising from unexpected funding

---

[10]Pub. L. No. 111-203, § 165, 124 Stat. 1376, 1423 (2010) (codified at 12 U.S.C. § 5365).

[11]This inherent vulnerability arises from the role of banks in using deposits that are available upon demand to fund long-term, illiquid loans.

[12]The Federal Reserve System consists of the Federal Reserve Board—a federal agency—and 12 regional Reserve Banks. The Federal Reserve Board has delegated some of its responsibilities for supervision and regulation to the Reserve Banks. The Federal Reserve Act authorizes the Reserve Banks to make discount window loans to the extent authorized by the Federal Reserve Board. Pub. L. No. 63-43, §§ 10B, 13, 38 Stat. 251 (codified at of 12 U.S.C. §§ 347b(a), 343).

pressures. In a financial crisis, discount window lending can provide broader liquidity support to the banking system that can help mitigate strains in financial markets. The Federal Reserve Board authorizes the Reserve Banks to offer three discount window programs to depository institutions: primary credit, secondary credit, and seasonal credit, each with its own terms.[13] The primary credit program is the principal discount window program and extends credit to depository institutions in generally sound condition on a very short-term basis (usually overnight). The secondary credit program is available to extend credit on a very short-term basis for depository institutions that are not eligible for primary credit, with the purpose of helping institutions to return to market sources of funds. The seasonal credit program generally extends loans to small depository institutions that face seasonal fluctuations in their funding needs. Section 10B of the Federal Reserve Act provides the statutory framework for these programs and, among other things, requires all discount window loans to be secured to the satisfaction of the lending Reserve Bank.[14]

Deposit Insurance

FDIC deposit insurance covers deposit accounts—including checking and savings accounts, money market deposit accounts, and certificates of deposit—at insured depository institutions up to the insurance limit and is backed by the full faith and credit of the U.S. government. Federal deposit insurance was created to reduce the incentive for depositors to withdraw funds from banks during a financial panic and maintain stability and confidence in the nation's banking system. During the 1800s and early 1900s, a number of states adopted different versions of deposit insurance to insure bank obligations in response to a wave of bank failures. However, these state insurance funds were later unable to cope with economic events during the 1920s, which led to calls for a system of federal deposit insurance to maintain financial stability. The Banking Act of 1933, which created FDIC by an amendment to the Federal Reserve Act, authorized FDIC to provide deposit insurance to banks and went into effect on January 1, 1934.[15] The deposit insurance fund, administered by FDIC to resolve failed banks and thrifts, protects depositors from losses due to institution failures up to a limit. The deposit insurance fund is

---

[13]12 C.F.R. § 201.4(a)-(c).

[14]12 U.S.C. § 347b(a).

[15]Pub. L. No. 73-66, 48 Stat. 162 (codified in scattered sections of 12 U.S.C.). The Banking Act of 1933 is also known as the Glass-Steagall Act.

GAO-14-18 Government Support for Bank Holding Companies

primarily funded by fees from assessments on insured depository institutions. If necessary, FDIC can borrow from Treasury, the Federal Financing Bank, and the Federal Home Loan Banks. As discussed later in this report, the Dodd-Frank Act permanently increased the deposit insurance limit from $100,000 to $250,000 and changed the base used to determine an insured depository institution's risk-based assessment to be paid into the deposit insurance fund.[16]

Emergency Authorities

In addition to the discount window and deposit insurance, during the 2007-2009 financial crisis the Federal Reserve Board and FDIC used their emergency authorities to assist individual failing institutions. As discussed later in this report, the Dodd-Frank Act changed these authorities so that emergency lending can no longer be provided to assist a single and specific firm but rather can only be made available through a program with broad-based eligibility—that is, a program that provides funding support to institutions that meet program requirements and choose to participate.[17]

- *Federal Reserve emergency lending authority.* Prior to the Dodd-Frank Act, emergency lending authority under Section 13(3) of the Federal Reserve Act permitted the Federal Reserve Board, in unusual and exigent circumstances, to authorize a Reserve Bank to extend credit to individuals, partnerships, or corporations, if the Reserve Bank determined that adequate credit was not available from other banking institutions, and if the extension of credit was secured to the satisfaction of the lending Reserve Bank.[18] During the financial crisis of 2007-2009, the Federal Reserve Board invoked this authority on a number of occasions to authorize one or more Reserve Banks to provide emergency assistance to particular institutions or to establish new programs to provide liquidity support to important credit markets.

- *FDIC open bank assistance.* The FDIC Improvement Act of 1991 included a systemic risk exception to the requirement that FDIC resolve failed banks using the least costly method.[19] Under this

---

[16]Pub. L. No. 111-203, §§ 331, 334-335, 124 Stat. 1376, 1538-40 (2010).

[17]§1101(a), 124 Stat. at 2113.

[18]Pub. L. No. 63-43, § 13(3), 38 Stat. 251 (codified at 12 U.S.C. § 343).

[19]Pub. L. No. 102-242, § 141, 105 Stat. 2236, 2275 (codified at 12 U.S.C. § 1823(c)(4)(G)).

exception, FDIC could provide assistance to a failing bank if compliance with its requirements to resolve the bank using the least costly approach would have "serious adverse effects on economic conditions and financial stability"—that is, would cause systemic risk—and if such assistance would "avoid or mitigate such adverse effects."[20] FDIC could act under the exception only under a process that included recommendations from the FDIC Board of Directors and Federal Reserve Board and approval by the Treasury Secretary.[21] The agencies invoked this authority during the crisis to authorize FDIC to provide guarantees to particular banks and to introduce new guarantee programs with broad-based eligibility. As discussed later in this report, the Dodd-Frank Act effectively removed FDIC's authority to provide assistance to failing banks outside of a receivership.

Federal Home Loan Bank System

The Federal Home Loan Bank (FHLB) System also serves to provide funding support to depository institutions during normal and strained market conditions. The FHLB System is a government-sponsored enterprise (GSE) that consists of 12 Federal Home Loan Banks (FHLB) and is cooperatively owned by member financial institutions, which include banks, thrifts, insurance companies, and credit unions. The primary mission of the FHLB System is to promote housing and community development by making loans, known as advances, to member financial institutions. These institutions are required to secure FHLB advances with high-quality collateral (such as single-family mortgages) and may use FHLB advances to fund mortgages. To raise the funds necessary to carry out its activities, the FHLB System issues debt in the capital markets at favorable rates compared to commercial borrowings due to market perceptions that the federal government would intervene to support the FHLB System in a crisis, thereby reducing its risk of default. When credit markets become strained, as they did during the most recent crisis, the FHLB System can serve as an important backup source of liquidity for member institutions that meet the FHLBs' collateral and other requirements.

---

[20]Id.

[21]Id. For more information about this the systemic risk exception, see GAO, *Federal Deposit Insurance Act: Regulators' Use of Systemic Risk Exception Raises Moral Hazard Concerns and Opportunities Exist to Clarify the Provision*, GAO-10-100 (Washington, D.C.: Apr. 15, 2010).

2007-2009 Financial Crisis

The 2007-2009 financial crisis was the most severe that the United States has experienced since the Great Depression. The dramatic decline in the U.S. housing market that began in 2006 precipitated a decline in the price of financial assets that were associated with housing, particularly mortgage-related assets based on subprime loans. Some institutions found themselves so exposed to declines in the values of these assets that they were threatened with failure—and some failed—because they were unable to raise the necessary capital as the value of their lending and securities portfolios declined. Uncertainty about the financial condition and solvency of financial entities led banks to dramatically raise the interest rates they charged each other for funds and, in late 2008, interbank lending effectively came to a halt. The same uncertainty also led money market funds, pension funds, hedge funds, and other entities that provide funds to financial institutions to raise their interest rates, shorten their terms, and tighten credit standards. As their funding became increasingly difficult to obtain, financial institutions responded by raising the prices and tightening their credit standards for lending to households and nonfinancial businesses. The liquidity and credit crisis made the financing on which businesses and individuals depend increasingly difficult to obtain as cash-strapped banks tightened underwriting standards, resulting in a contraction of credit to the economy. By late summer of 2008, the potential ramifications of the financial crisis included the continued failure of financial institutions, increased losses of individual wealth, reduced corporate investments, and further tightening of credit that would exacerbate the emerging global economic slowdown that was beginning to take shape.

Because financial crises can result in severe damage to the economy and the road to recovery can be long, governments and monetary authorities have historically undertaken interventions, even though some of the resulting actions raise concerns about moral hazard and can pose a risk of losses to taxpayers.[22] Given its severity and systemic nature, the recent global financial crisis prompted substantial interventions starting in late 2007, after problems in the subprime mortgage market intensified. As discussed further in the next section of this report, these interventions included the creation of temporary government programs to support

---

[22]For a more detailed discussion of the economic losses associated with the 2007-2009 financial crisis, see GAO, *Financial Regulatory Reform: Financial Crisis Losses and Potential Impacts of the Dodd-Frank Act*, GAO-13-180 (Washington, D.C.: Jan. 16, 2013).

GAO-14-18 Government Support for Bank Holding Companies

important credit markets and financial institutions that intermediate credit in the economy by channeling funds from savers to borrowers.

Government Actions to Stabilize Markets Resulted in Significant Support to Bank Holding Companies

From 2007 through 2009, the federal government's actions to stabilize the financial system provided funding support and other benefits to bank holding companies and their bank and nonbank financial subsidiaries. The Federal Reserve Board, Treasury, and FDIC introduced new programs with broad-based eligibility that provided funding support to institutions that met program requirements and chose to participate.[23] Selected programs—for which eligibility was not restricted exclusively to institutions that were part of a bank holding company—included Federal Reserve System lending programs, Treasury capital investment programs, and FDIC programs that guaranteed uninsured deposits and new debt issues. Isolating the impact of individual interventions is difficult, but collectively these actions likely improved financial conditions by enhancing confidence in financial institutions and the financial system. Bank holding companies and their subsidiaries also accrued benefits specific to their own institutions, including liquidity benefits from programs that allowed them to borrow at lower interest rates and at longer maturities than might have been available in the markets. Programs generally were made available to institutions of various sizes, and differences in the use of programs by institutions of various sizes were driven in part by differences in how institutions funded themselves. For example, compared to smaller bank holding companies, larger bank holding companies relied less on deposits as a source of funding and more on short-term credit markets and participated more in programs created to stabilize these markets. At the end of 2008, use of these programs—measured for each institution as the percentage of total assets supported by the programs—was larger on average for larger banking organizations—those with $50 billion or more in total assets—than for smaller banking organizations. The six largest bank holding companies were significant participants in several emergency programs but exited most of the programs by the end of 2009. Differences in program use across banking organizations of various sizes diminished as

---

[23]This report focuses on those emergency programs that provided the most significant direct funding support to bank holding companies or their subsidiaries. As a result, we do not include an analysis of the Term Asset-Backed Securities Loan Facility, or the Public-Private Investment Partnership, among others, because these programs did not provide significant *direct* support to bank holding companies or their subsidiaries.

institutions exited the programs. In addition to programs that provided broad-based support, the Federal Reserve Board granted a number of regulatory exemptions to allow banks to provide liquidity support to their nonbank affiliates and for other purposes. Finally, some large bank holding companies benefitted from individual institution assistance or regulatory relief. For example, government assistance to prevent the failures of large institutions benefited recipients of this assistance and other market participants.

Crisis Programs with Broad-Based Eligibility Provided Funding Support to Bank Holding Companies and Their Subsidiaries

During the financial crisis, the Federal Reserve System, Treasury, and FDIC introduced new programs with broad-based eligibility to provide general funding support to the financial sector and to stabilize the financial system. Given this report's focus on bank holding companies, this section focuses on the financial stability programs that provided the most significant funding support directly to bank holding companies or their bank or nonbank subsidiaries. Table 1 provides an overview of the size, purpose, terms, and conditions of these programs, which included:

- the Federal Reserve System's Term Auction Facility (TAF); Primary Dealer Credit Facility (PDCF); Term Securities Lending Facility (TSLF); and Commercial Paper Funding Facility (CPFF);
- Treasury's Capital Purchase Program (CPP); and
- FDIC's Temporary Liquidity Guarantee Program (TLGP), which had two components: the Debt Guarantee Program (DGP) guaranteed certain newly issued senior unsecured debt, and the Transaction Account Guarantee Program (TAGP) guaranteed certain previously uninsured deposits.

Institutions eligible for these programs included both entities that were part of a bank holding company structure and entities that were not. The Federal Reserve System designed its emergency programs to address disruptions to particular credit markets and to assist participants in these markets. For example, the Federal Reserve System's programs that targeted support to repurchase agreement markets provided assistance to securities firms that were subsidiaries of bank holding companies and securities firms that were not. The Federal Reserve System's CPFF purchased commercial paper from participating bank holding companies and other financial and nonfinancial firms that met the program's eligibility requirements. Treasury's CPP and FDIC's TLGP provided support primarily to insured depository institutions (banks and thrifts) and bank and savings and loan holding companies.

Table 1: Overview of Largest Emergency Programs That Provided General Funding Support to Bank Holding Companies or Their Subsidiaries

Dollars in billions

Programs	Peak dollar amount	Purpose	Key terms
Federal Reserve System			
TAF – Term Auction Facility[a] (Dec. 12, 2007–Mar. 8, 2010)	$493	Auctioned 1 and 3-month discount window loans to depository institutions to address strains in term interbank lending markets.	*Eligible Institutions.* Depository institutions eligible for the primary credit discount window program and expected to remain so over the TAF loan term.[b] *Interest rate.* The interest rate was determined by auction. For each auction, winning bidders were awarded loans at the same interest rate. *Collateral eligibility.* Based on discount window requirements.[c]
PDCF - Primary Dealer Credit Facility (Mar. 16, 2008–Feb. 1, 2010)	$130	Provided overnight cash loans to primary dealers against eligible collateral to address strains in the repurchase agreement markets.	*Eligible institutions.* Primary dealers, a designated group of broker-dealers and banks that transacted with the Federal Reserve Bank of New York in its conduct of open market operations.[d] *Interest rate and fees.* The interest rate was equal to the primary credit rate - the rate charged on discount window loans in the primary credit program. The Federal Reserve Bank of New York charged a frequency-based fee, ranging from 10 to 40 basis points, to dealers who accessed the facility on more than 45 out of 180 business days. *Collateral eligibility.* Initially limited to collateral eligible for open market operations (e.g., Treasury and agency securities) as well as investment-grade corporate securities, municipal securities, and asset-backed securities (ABS); later expanded to include all securities eligible to be pledged in the triparty repurchase agreements system, including noninvestment grade securities and equities
TSLF - Term Securities Lending Facility (Mar. 11, 2008–Feb. 1, 2010)	$236	Auctioned loans of U.S. Treasury securities to primary dealers against eligible collateral to address strains in the repurchase agreement markets.	*Eligible institutions.* Primary dealers (same as PDCF) *Interest rate.* The interest rate was determined by auction (similar to TAF). For each auction, winning bidders were awarded loans at the same interest rate. *Collateral eligibility.* TSLF auctioned loans of securities against two schedules of collateral. Schedule 1 included all collateral eligible for open market operations. Schedule 2 collateral initially included Schedule 1 collateral as well as highly-rated mortgage-backed securities (MBS). Schedule 2 collateral was later expanded to include investment grade corporate and municipal securities, MBS, and ABS.

Dollars in billions

Programs	Peak dollar amount	Purpose	Key terms
CPFF - Commercial Paper Funding Facility (Oct. 7, 2008–Feb. 1, 2010)	$348	Purchased asset-backed commercial paper (ABCP) and unsecured commercial paper from eligible issuers.	*Eligible issuers.* All U.S. issuers (including those with a foreign parent) with eligible commercial paper. To be eligible, commercial paper was required to have received the highest rating from at least one major credit rating agency.
			Interest rate. The interest rate was set at a fixed spread above the daily 3-month overnight indexed swap (OIS) rate to control for changes in short-term interest rates.[e] This spread was 100 basis points for unsecured commercial paper and 300 basis points for ABCP.
			Credit surcharge. To provide additional loss protection, issuers of unsecured paper were required to pay a credit surcharge of 100 basis points. Commercial paper issues guaranteed by TLGP were exempt from the surcharge.
Department of the Treasury (Treasury)			
CPP - Capital Purchase Program (Oct. 14, 2008–Dec. 31, 2009)	$205	The first and largest initiative under Treasury's Troubled Asset Relief Program; provided capital to eligible financial institutions by purchasing preferred shares and subordinated debt.	*Eligible institutions.* Qualifying institutions generally included U.S.-controlled depository institutions, bank holding companies, and most savings and loan holding companies.
			Dividends. Senior preferred shares paid dividends at a rate of 5 percent annually for the first 5 years and 9 percent annually thereafter. Treasury also received warrants to purchase shares of stock or a senior debt instrument.
			Interest on subordinated debt. For certain issuers, Treasury received subordinated debt rather than preferred shares to protect these institutions' special tax status. Interest rates for this debt were set at 7.7 percent for the first 5 years and 13.8 percent for the remaining years.
Federal Deposit Insurance Corporation (FDIC)			
TLGP – Temporary Liquidity Guarantee Program[f] (Announced Oct. 14, 2008) • DGP – Debt Guarantee Program (Guarantees expired Dec. 31, 2012) • TAGP – Transaction Account Guarantee Program (Expired Dec. 31, 2010)[g]	Approx. $346 debt and approx. $835 deposits	DGP guaranteed certain newly-issued senior unsecured debt of eligible institutions to improve liquidity in term funding markets. TAGP temporarily extended an unlimited deposit guarantee to domestic noninterest-bearing transaction accounts at participating insured depository institutions to limit further outflows of these deposits.	*Eligible institutions.* FDIC insured depository institutions (IDI); U.S. bank and savings and loan holding companies; and affiliates of IDIs upon application. *DGP fees.* FDIC assessed fees on each DGP-guaranteed debt issuance based on time to maturity. Following extensions of the DGP, FDIC also assessed surcharges. Surcharges for holding companies and affiliates of IDIs were twice as high as those for IDIs. *TAGP fees.* FDIC assessed a fee of 10 basis points on the quarter-end balance of eligible deposits over $250,000. Beginning in 2010, FDIC instead assessed risk-based fees of 15, 20, or 25 basis points of quarter-end balances over $250,000.

Source: FDIC, Federal Reserve System, and Treasury documents.

Note: This table includes the emergency programs that provided the most significant funding support directly to bank holding companies and their subsidiaries. Bank holding companies and their subsidiaries benefited from other emergency government programs, such as programs that assisted money market mutual funds. Dates in parentheses are the program announcement dates, and where relevant, the date the program or assistance was closed or terminated. The peak dollar amount

GAO-14-18 Government Support for Bank Holding Companies

shown for CPP represents the total dollar amount invested through CPP. For all other programs, the peak dollar amount shown represents the peak dollar amount outstanding.

[a]12 C.F.R. § 201.4(e).

[b]U.S. branches and agencies of foreign institutions that met program requirements were eligible to participate in TAF. The Reserve Banks extend discount window credit to U.S. depository institutions (including U.S. branches and agencies of foreign banks) under three programs, one of which is the primary credit program. Primary credit is available to generally sound depository institutions, typically on an overnight basis. To assess whether a depository institution is in sound financial condition, its Reserve Bank can regularly review the institution's condition, using supervisory ratings and data on adequacy of the institution's capital.

[c]TAF loans were collateralized based on haircut requirements for the discount window program. For TAF loans, Reserve Banks accepted as collateral any assets that were elig ble to secure discount window loans.

[d]Several primary dealers were subsidiaries of large U.S. bank holding companies or large foreign banking organizations. U.S. bank holding companies with primary dealer subsidiaries included Citigroup Inc., Bank of America Corporation, Goldman Sachs Group, Inc., JP Morgan Chase & Co., and Morgan Stanley. Goldman Sachs Group, Inc. and Morgan Stanley were not bank holding companies when PDCF and TSLF launched in March 2008, but both firms participated in these programs after they converted to bank holding companies in September 2008.

[e]The OIS rate is an interest rate that tracks expectations of the future federal funds rate.

[f]12 C.F.R. § 370.

[g]The Dodd-Frank Act provided temporary unlimited deposit insurance coverage for noninterest-bearing transaction accounts at all FDIC-insured institutions from December 31, 2010 through December 31, 2012. This coverage essentially was similar to that offered by TAGP. Pub. L. No. 111-203, § 343, 124 Stat. 1376, 1544 (2010).

Bank holding companies also benefited from other government programs, such as programs that targeted support to other market participants. For example, in the absence of Treasury and Federal Reserve System programs to guarantee and support money market mutual funds, respectively, such funds may have reduced their purchases of money market instruments issued by subsidiaries of bank holding companies and other firms, thereby exacerbating funding pressures on these firms. Other significant government programs included the Term Asset-Backed Securities Loan Facility (TALF), which was created by the Federal Reserve System to support certain securitization markets, and other programs created by Treasury under TARP authority.[24]

While the Federal Reserve System and FDIC provided expanded support through traditional safety net programs for insured banks during the crisis,

---

[24]For more information about TALF, see GAO, *Troubled Asset Relief Program: Treasury Needs to Strengthen Its Decision-Making Process on the Term Asset-Backed Securities Loan Facility*, GAO-10-25 (Washington, D.C.: Feb. 5, 2010). For more information about CPP and other TARP programs, see GAO, *Troubled Asset Relief Program: One Year Later, Actions Are Needed to Address Remaining Transparency and Accountability Challenges*, GAO-10-16 (Washington, D.C.: Oct. 8, 2009).

some of the emergency government programs provided funding support at the bank holding company level—where it could be used to support both bank and nonbank subsidiaries—or directly to nonbank entities. In late 2007, the Federal Reserve Board took a series of actions to ease strains in interbank funding markets, including lowering the target federal funds rate, easing terms at the discount window, and introducing a new program—TAF—to auction term loans to banks.[25] However, in part due to statutory and regulatory restrictions on the ability of insured banks to provide funding support to their nonbank affiliates, agencies determined that emergency government support to insured banks was not sufficient to stem disruptions to important credit markets. Nonbank credit markets—such as repurchase agreement and debt securities markets—had grown to rival the traditional banking sector in facilitating loans to consumers and businesses, and agencies determined that actions to address disruptions to these markets were needed to avert adverse impacts to the broader economy. For example, in March 2008, the Federal Reserve Board authorized PDCF and TSLF to address strains in repurchase agreement markets by providing emergency loans to broker-dealers, a few of whom were owned by U.S. bank holding companies.[26] When the crisis intensified in September 2008 following the failure of Lehman Brothers Holdings Inc.—a large broker-dealer holding company—the Federal Reserve Board modified terms for its existing programs and took other actions to expand funding support for both bank and nonbank entities.[27]

---

[25]To ease stresses in these markets, on August 17, 2007, the Federal Reserve Board approved two temporary changes to discount window terms: (1) a reduction of the discount rate—the interest rate at which the Reserve Banks extended collateralized loans at the discount window—by 50 basis points; and (2) an extension of the discount window lending term from overnight to up to 30 days, with the possibility of renewal. One basis point is equivalent to 0.01 percent or 1/100th of a percent. On March 16, 2008, the Federal Reserve Board further reduced the spread of the primary credit rate over the target federal funds rate to 25 basis points and increased the maximum maturity of discount window loans to 90 days.

[26]In March 2008, U.S. bank holding companies with primary dealer subsidiaries included Citigroup, Inc., Bank of America Corporation, and JP Morgan Chase & Co. Morgan Stanley and Goldman Sachs Group Inc. also had subsidiaries that were primary dealers and in September 2008, both firms converted to bank holding companies.

[27]On September 14, 2008, the Federal Reserve Board announced that TSLF-eligible collateral would be expanded to include all investment-grade debt securities and PDCF-eligible collateral would be expanded to include all securities eligible to be pledged in the triparty repurchase agreements system, including noninvestment-grade securities and equities. On September 29, 2008, the Federal Reserve Board also announced expanded support through TAF by doubling the amount of funds that would be available in each TAF auction cycle from $150 billion to $300 billion.

In September 2008, Treasury and the Federal Reserve System introduced new temporary programs to address liquidity pressures on money market funds and to help ensure that these funds could continue to purchase money market instruments issued by bank holding companies and other firms.[28] In addition, in October 2008, Congress enacted legislation under which Treasury provided capital investments to banks, bank holding companies, and other institutions; the legislation also temporarily increased FDIC's deposit insurance limit from $100,000 to $250,000.[29] Also that month, the Federal Reserve System created CPFF to support commercial paper markets, and FDIC introduced TLGP, under which it guaranteed previously uninsured transaction accounts and certain newly issued senior unsecured debt for participating insured depository institutions, bank and savings and loan holding companies, and approved affiliates of insured depository institutions. For a more detailed discussion of the circumstances surrounding the creation of these programs, see appendix II.

Isolating the impact of individual government interventions is difficult, but collectively these interventions helped to improve financial conditions by enhancing confidence in financial institutions and the financial system overall.[30] Bank holding companies and their subsidiaries, in addition to

---

[28]In September 2008, following the failure of Lehman Brothers Holdings Inc., many money market mutual funds faced severe liquidity pressures as redemption requests from their investors increased significantly. Treasury and Federal Reserve Board officials became concerned that pressures on these funds could further exacerbate turmoil in the markets, as these funds were significant investors in many money market instruments, such as commercial paper and certificates of deposit. On September 19, 2008, Treasury announced that it would insure the holdings of any publicly offered eligible money market mutual fund—both retail and institutional—that paid a fee to participate in the program. On the same day, the Federal Reserve Board authorized the creation of a new program—the AMLF—to provide liquidity support to money market mutual funds and to promote liquidity in the ABCP markets. AMLF provided loans to U.S. depository institutions, their holding companies, and affiliates that used the proceeds of these loans to purchase ABCP from money market mutual funds. For more information about AMLF, see GAO, *Federal Reserve System: Opportunities Exist to Strengthen Policies and Processes for Managing Emergency Assistance,* GAO-11-696 (Washington, D.C.: July 21, 2011).

[29]Emergency Economic Stabilization Act of 2008, Pub. L. No. 110-343, Div. A, 122 Stat. 3765 (12 U.S.C. §§ 5201-5261).

[30]In prior work, we found that TARP, along with other efforts by the Federal Reserve System and FDIC, made important contributions to helping stabilize credit markets. For example, the TED spread—a key indicator of credit risk that gauges the willingness of banks to lend to other banks—had narrowed to precrisis levels within a year of the October 2008 announcements of TARP, TLGP, CPFF, and other government actions.

the financial sector and the economy as a whole, benefited from improved financial conditions. Bank holding companies and their subsidiaries also experienced individual benefits from participating in particular programs.

Individually and collectively, government lending, guarantee, and capital programs provided important liquidity and other benefits to bank holding companies and their subsidiaries including:

- **Access to funding in quantities and/or at prices that were generally not available in the markets**. Government entities generally sought to set prices for assistance through these programs to be less expensive than prices available during crisis conditions but more expensive than prices available during normal market conditions.[31] In some credit markets assisted by government programs—such as commercial paper and repurchase agreement markets—conditions had deteriorated such that many institutions faced substantially reduced access to these markets or had no access at all. As discussed below, we compared program pricing to relevant indicators of market pricing where available and found that emergency lending and guarantee programs generally were priced below market alternatives that may have been available. The availability of funding support at this pricing in predictable quantities was also beneficial. Even at times when eligible institutions did not access the available programs, these programs diversified the sources of funds that could be available to them if they faced increased funding pressures.

- **Access to funding at longer maturities**. By providing and standing ready to provide funding support for terms of 1 month or longer, government programs helped to reduce rollover risk—the risk that an institution would be unable to renew or "rollover" funding obligations as they came due—for individual institutions and their counterparties. At times during the crisis, bank holding companies and their subsidiaries faced difficulties borrowing at terms of 1 month or longer in several important credit markets, including interbank, repurchase agreement, and commercial paper markets. Government programs mitigated funding pressures for borrowers in these markets by reducing the risk that funding sources would rapidly disappear for an institution or its counterparties. Because participants in these

---

[31]This pricing was intended to encourage program participants to exit the programs as market conditions normalized.

programs were also lenders of funds, these programs helped to encourage these institutions to continue to lend funds to support the economy.

- **Stabilizing deposit funding**. FDIC's TAGP, which temporarily insured certain previously uninsured deposits for a fee, helped to stabilize deposit funding by removing the risk of loss from deposit accounts that were commonly used to meet payroll and other business transaction purposes and allowing banks, particularly smaller ones, to retain these accounts. Deposits are the primary source of funding for most banks, and smaller banks tend to fund themselves to a greater extent with deposits.

- **Funding support for a broad range of collateral types**. A few Federal Reserve System programs provided important liquidity benefits to individual institutions and credit markets by allowing institutions to obtain liquidity against a broad range of collateral types. TAF provided 1-month and 3-month loans to eligible banks against collateral types that could also be used to secure discount window loans. While TAF collateral requirements were based on discount window requirements, TAF provided emergency credit on a much larger scale, with TAF loans outstanding peaking at nearly $500 billion, compared to peak primary credit outstanding during the crisis of just over $100 billion.[32] In March 2008, the Federal Reserve System began providing liquidity support to certain nonbank financial firms—the primary dealers—for less liquid collateral types through PDCF and TSLF. Through PDCF, the Federal Reserve Bank of New York (FRBNY) allowed primary dealers to obtain overnight cash loans against harder-to-value collateral types, such as mortgage-backed securities. Through TSLF, FRBNY auctioned loans of Treasury securities to primary dealers in exchange for less-liquid collateral types to increase the amount of high-quality collateral these dealers had available to borrow against in repurchase agreement markets. When pressures in repurchase agreement markets intensified in September 2008, the Federal Reserve Board expanded the types of collateral it accepted for both PDCF and TSLF.

---

[32]Because of the perceived stigma associated with borrowing from the discount window, banks that participated in TAF might have been reluctant to turn to the discount window for funding support.

Although imperfect, one indicator of the extent to which an institution directly benefited from participation in an emergency program is the relative price of estimated market alternatives to the program. To determine how pricing of the emergency assistance compared to market rates, we compared pricing for programs to the pricing for market alternatives that might have been available to program participants. First, we compared the interest rates and fees charged by the Federal Reserve System and FDIC for participation in the emergency lending and guarantee programs with available market alternatives. We considered a number of potential indicators of market interest rates available to financial institutions, including a survey of interbank interest rates (the London Interbank Offered Rate or LIBOR), commercial paper interest rates published by the Federal Reserve Board, spreads on bank credit default swaps (CDS) and interest rates on repurchase agreements. These interest rates provide a general indication of market alternatives that could have been available to participants, but for a number of reasons the rates are unlikely to reflect available alternatives for all participants at all points in time during the crisis and cannot be used to produce a precise quantification of the benefits that accrued to participating financial institutions.[33] For example, participants' access to market alternatives may have been limited, data on the relevant private market may be limited, or market alternatives could vary across participants in ways that we do not observe in the data. The markets targeted by emergency programs had experienced significant strains, such as a substantial drop in liquidity, a sharp increase in prices, or lenders restricting access only to the most credit worthy borrowers or accepting only the safest collateral. Also, our indicators do not capture all of the benefits associated with participation in the relevant programs. Furthermore, once programs were introduced, they probably influenced the price of market alternatives, making it difficult to interpret differences

---

[33]In our analysis, we discarded values of spreads between program pricing and market alternatives when they were zero or negative—negative spreads are unlikely to capture the benefits that accrued to participants. For example, we excluded 15 observations (or 40 percent of auctions) in our analysis of TSLF when the schedule 1 auction rate was equal to or above the private cost for similar borrowing but did not exclude any observations in our analysis of DGP because the DGP fee never exceeded the weighted-average private cost for similar guarantees during the time period we analyzed. If these truly reflected market alternatives for the pool of potential participants then there would be no participation, or the participation would have been based on other considerations. Participation by itself suggests that program prices and/or terms were relatively attractive in comparison to available alternatives—benefits could arise from price, quantity available, or other nonprice characteristics of the assistance (loan term, eligible collateral, etc.).

between emergency program and market prices while programs were active. Second, to determine the extent to which Treasury capital investment programs were priced more generously than market alternatives, we reviewed estimates of the expected budget cost associated with equity funding support programs as well as a valuation analysis commissioned by the Congressional Oversight Panel. For more details on our methodology for these analyses, see appendix III.

Based on our analysis, we found that emergency assistance provided through these programs was often priced below estimated market alternatives that might have been available to program participants. This result is consistent with a policy goal of these programs to stabilize financial markets and restore confidence in the financial sector. The pricing of emergency assistance below estimated market alternatives is also evidenced by the significant participation in these programs. Specifically, we found that emergency lending and guarantee programs were generally priced below certain indicators of market alternatives that could have been available. In addition, based on analyses we reviewed, Treasury paid prices above estimated market prices for emergency equity support programs. For selected programs that we analyzed, we also found that program pricing would likely have become unattractive in comparison to market pricing during normal and more stable credit conditions.

Federal Reserve System programs. Federal Reserve System emergency lending programs during the crisis provided sources of both secured and unsecured funding at rates that were often below those of potential market alternatives and at terms that reduced rollover risk for participants. These characteristics are consistent with a policy goal to stabilize financial conditions by providing funding support for financial institutions that relied on wholesale funding markets. At the time, the markets targeted by the Federal Reserve emergency programs had experienced strains, such as a drop in volume or a significant increase in prices or collateral standards.

- *TAF*. Interest rates on TAF loans, on average, were between 22 and 39 basis points lower than three market interest rates that could have represented alternatives for participants. TAF auctioned collateralized loans—generally at terms of either 28 or 84 days—to insured banks to help alleviate strains in term funding markets. We compared interest rates for 28-day TAF loans with 1-month LIBOR, 30-day asset-backed commercial paper (ABCP) rates, and interest rates on very large 1-month unsecured certificates of deposit.[34] We chose these interest rates because they are all indicators of the cost of borrowing for financial institutions in term funding markets. However each differs from TAF in important ways. For example, LIBOR is based on unsecured loans (TAF loans were secured by collateral) and ABCP, despite being secured, has other features that differ from TAF, including the mix of underlying collateral.[35] We found that LIBOR exceeded TAF interest rates by an average of 22 basis points. ABCP interest rates exceeded TAF interest rates by on average 39 basis points and interest rates on very large certificates of deposit exceeded TAF interest rates by on average 29 basis points while the program was active. Because of differences between TAF and these measures of market interest rates, these spreads are an imperfect measure of the extent to which banks derived benefits from participating in TAF.

- *PDCF.* Our analysis suggests that PDCF provided secured overnight funding on more favorable terms for some types of collateral (such as corporate debt) than market alternatives that some primary dealers might have relied upon in the absence of PDCF. Because PDCF operated in a similar manner to repurchase agreement markets, we compared PDCF terms to available data for triparty and bilateral repurchase agreement transactions.[36] One important term for repurchase agreement loans is the haircut, which is the amount of additional collateral the lender requires over the value of the loan.[37]

---

[34]We are aware that concerns about LIBOR manipulation could affect its usefulness as an indicator of potential market alternatives for banks. We discussed this issue with Federal Reserve Bank of New York officials who indicated that it was still among the best available indicators despite these concerns. In addition, GAO has found in previous work that LIBOR reflected significant financial market stress during the 2007-2009 financial crisis. See GAO-10-16.

[35]In addition, there can be uncertainty about the assets underlying ABCP or limited liquidity support from sponsors.

[36]Triparty repurchase agreement transactions are intermediated by a third party (a clearing bank) that stands between the borrower and lender.

[37]Interest rates are another important term for repurchase loans. However, we were unable to compare PDCF interest rates to market alternatives for all eligible collateral types because available data for repurchase agreement market interest rates are limited to higher quality and more liquid collateral types (such as Treasury securities). While repurchase agreement lenders generally require higher interest rates for riskier and less liquid collateral types, PDCF offered loans at the same interest rate for all collateral types.

GAO-14-18 Government Support for Bank Holding Companies

Repurchase agreement lenders generally require higher haircuts on riskier and less liquid collateral types. PDCF offered loans at the same interest rate (the discount rate charged on discount window loans) for all collateral types and applied a haircut schedule that assigned progressively higher haircuts to riskier assets. We compared PDCF haircuts to market haircuts for selected asset classes in the triparty repurchase agreement market. We found that the haircut required by PDCF was consistently greater than the median haircut in the triparty repurchase agreement market for comparable asset classes. Thus, borrowers who faced the median haircut on their collateral in the triparty market were better off borrowing in the triparty market than through PDCF, all else being equal. However, the PDCF haircut was smaller than the 75th percentile haircut in the triparty market for a variety of collateral types. This implies that higher-risk borrowers were better off borrowing through PDCF than through the triparty market, at least for certain types of collateral. Smaller haircuts would have allowed these PDCF participants to borrow more against the same collateral than in private repurchase agreement markets.

- *TSLF*. TSLF allowed primary dealers to obtain funding for the most commonly pledged collateral types at 32 basis points below an estimated market alternative. When TSLF was created in March 2008, repurchase agreement lenders were requiring higher interest rates and haircuts for loans against a range of less-liquid collateral types and were reluctant to lend against mortgage-related securities.[38] Through TSLF, primary dealers paid an auction-determined interest rate to exchange harder-to-finance collateral for more liquid Treasury securities—which were easier to borrow against in repurchase agreement markets—generally for a term of 28 days. TSLF held separate auctions of Treasury securities against two different schedules of collateral to apply a higher interest rate to riskier collateral. Schedule 1 collateral included higher quality assets, such as agency debt and agency mortgage-backed securities (MBS), and Schedule 2 collateral included Schedule 1 collateral and a broader range of asset types, such as highly-rated private-label MBS. We compared TSLF interest rates to the difference between lower interest rates primary dealers might have paid on repurchase agreements secured by Treasury securities and the higher interest rates they

---

[38]As a result, many financial institutions increasingly had to rely on higher quality collateral, such as Treasury securities, to obtain cash in these markets, and a shortage of such high-quality collateral emerged.

could have paid on repurchase agreements secured by TSLF-eligible collateral. Due to limited availability of interest rate data for repurchase agreements collateralized by other lower-quality collateral eligible for TSLF, such as private-label MBS, we compared TSLF interest rates to the difference or spread between interest rates on repurchase agreements collateralized by agency MBS and repurchase agreements collateralized by Treasury securities.[39] We found that the spread between repurchase agreement interest rates on agency MBS (the most commonly-pledged collateral for TSLF) and Treasury securities exceeded TSLF interest rates by on average 32 basis points while the program was active.[40]

- *CPFF*. CPFF purchased 3-month commercial paper at prices that were lower than market rates during the crisis on instruments that could have represented alternative funding sources but were more expensive than average commercial paper rates during normal market conditions. CPFF controlled for changes in short-term interest rates by setting the price of commercial paper issuance to CPFF at a fixed spread above the daily 3-month overnight indexed swap rate, a rate that tracks investor expectations about the future federal funds rate. Table 2 summarizes the pricing structure for CPFF. We compared all-in borrowing costs (an interest rate plus a credit surcharge for unsecured borrowing) for CPFF borrowers with 3-month LIBOR. To determine how CPFF pricing compared to borrowing costs in crisis conditions, we compared CPFF pricing terms to 3-month LIBOR for the period from the failure of Lehman Brothers Holdings Inc. (Sept. 14, 2008) through the date on which CPFF became operational (Oct. 27, 2008). We found that average CPFF pricing terms were lower than the average LIBOR rate by 92 basis points and 44 basis points for CPFF purchases of unsecured commercial paper and collateralized ABCP, respectively. To determine how unsecured CPFF rates compared to benchmarks for borrowing costs in normal market conditions, we applied the CPFF pricing rule for unsecured commercial paper to a 2-month period in 2006 and found that CPFF pricing would have been more expensive than AA unsecured

---

[39]As a result we could only compare market repurchase agreement interest rates with interest rates from the Schedule 1 auctions.

[40]Researchers at the Federal Reserve Bank of New York also found that TSLF was priced below estimated market rates, although the size of the difference they estimated was smaller than our results.

commercial paper interest rates by roughly 200 basis points and LIBOR by over 190 basis points. This analysis suggests that CPFF would have become less attractive to participants as market conditions improved.

Table 2: Pricing Terms for Commercial Paper Funding Facility

Rates and fees	Unsecured commercial paper	ABCP
Interest rate	3-month OIS + 100 basis points	3-month OIS + 300 basis points
Credit surcharge	100 basis points	None
All-in-cost	3-month OIS + 200 basis points	3-month OIS + 300 basis points

Source: Federal Reserve Board.

Treasury capital investments. Analyses we reviewed suggest that the prices Treasury paid for equity in financial institutions participating in TARP exceeded estimated market prices that private investors might have paid for comparable investments in these institutions during the crisis. This pricing is consistent with a policy goal to stabilize financial conditions by improving the equity capitalization of banks. In late 2008, before CPP was announced, banks had difficulty issuing sufficient new equity to investors. We reviewed estimates of the expected budget cost associated with Treasury's equity funding support programs under TARP, CPP and the Targeted Investment Program (TIP), as well as a valuation analysis commissioned by the Congressional Oversight Panel.[41] Some of the benefits that accrued to banks from participation in equity funding support programs are likely to be proportional to the expected budgetary cost (also known as subsidy rates) estimated for accounting purposes. Treasury and Congressional Budget Office estimates of subsidy rates are based on a net present value analysis—the price and terms which are offered by a federal agency are compared to the lifetime expected cost (net present value) of the equity, and the difference is known as a

---

[41]Through TIP, Treasury sought to foster market stability and strengthen the economy by making case-by-case investments in institutions that it deemed critical to the functioning of the financial system. Bank of America Corporation and Citigroup Inc. were the only two institutions that participated in this program.

subsidy. [42] The valuation analysis commissioned by the Congressional Oversight Panel explicitly compared the prices received by Treasury with market-based valuations of securities it determined to be comparable. Estimates of subsidy rates by Treasury, the Congressional Budget Office, and the Congressional Oversight Panel were generally similar for CPP, while the Congressional Budget Office's estimates for TIP were substantially lower than those of Treasury and the Congressional Oversight Panel (see fig. 1). Based on these three analyses, these estimated subsidy rates suggest that the prices Treasury paid for equity in financial institutions were 18 to 27 percent over estimated market prices for CPP and 26 to 50 percent over estimated market prices for TIP equity. Estimates reflect differences in timing, methodology, and institutions included in the analyses, which we discussed previously and in the note to figure 1. [43]

[42]Because private market participants might have charged a price based on a comparable net present value analysis, banks would have benefitted to the extent that the prices offered by Treasury for their equity exceed what they were likely to receive based on the net present value. We used the earliest available estimates from the Congressional Budget Office and Treasury as they were closest to market conditions at the time that programs were initiated. Estimates of these subsidy rates depended on timing and market conditions and the size of these subsidy rates l kely fell over time as market conditions improved.

[43]For more details on their respective methodologies, see Congressional Budget Office, *The Troubled Asset Relief Program: Report on Transactions Through December 31, 2008* (Washington, D.C.: January 2009); GAO-10-301; and Congressional Oversight Panel, *February Oversight Report: Valuing Treasury's Acquisitions* (Washington, D.C.: February 2009).

GAO-14-18 Government Support for Bank Holding Companies

Figure 1. Emergency Capital Program Subsidy Estimates

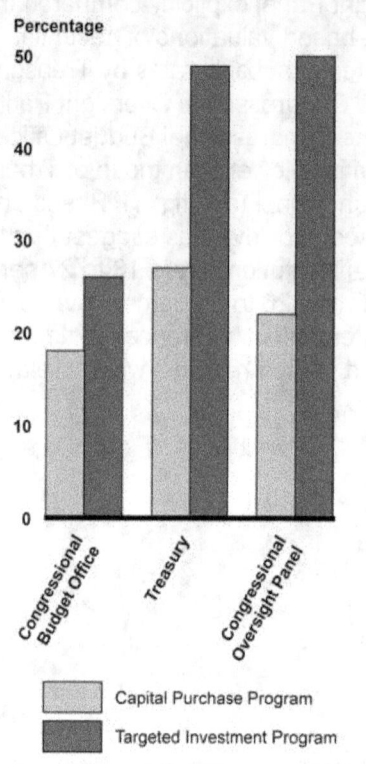

Source: GAO analysis of CBO, Treasury, and COP data.

Note: Analysis by the Congressional Budget Office is as of December 31, 2008, and the Targeted Investment Program (TIP) estimate includes only Citigroup. Treasury financial statement information is as of September 30, 2009. Analysis commissioned by the Congressional Oversight Panel includes valuations based on data from October 2008 through November 2008 and the TIP estimate includes only Citigroup, and the CPP estimate is based on a sample of 8 relatively large financial institutions. We used the earliest available estimates from the Congressional Budget Office and Treasury as they were closest to market conditions at the time that programs were initiated. Estimates of these subsidy rates depended on timing and market conditions and the size of these subsidy rates likely fell over time as market conditions improved.

FDIC's DGP. For the DGP guarantees that we analyzed, the fees for FDIC's DGP were on average 278 basis points below the private cost of similar guarantees during crisis conditions, but more expensive than similar guarantees that were available in the private market during normal credit conditions. This pricing is consistent with a policy goal to promote financial stability by improving access to sources of debt funding. FDIC's DGP provided guarantees for certain newly issued senior unsecured debt for banks, bank holding companies, and other eligible institutions. When DGP was created in October 2008, lending to financial institutions in public debt markets had dropped dramatically. The fees for participation

GAO-14-18 Government Support for Bank Holding Companies

in DGP were based on the maturity of guaranteed liabilities (the longer the maturity the higher the fee) and the type of financial institution. We analyzed the 100-basis point fee that DGP charged to guarantee debt with a maturity of 1 year, plus the 10-basis point premium charged to bank holding companies.[44] We compared the total DGP fee with the weighted average price of 1-year bank CDS for certain bank holding companies because the guarantee is essentially similar to a private party insuring against the risk of default using a CDS.[45] Our analysis covered the period from the failure of Lehman Brothers (in September 2008) through the date DGP became operational (in October 2008). We found that the cost of insuring against bank default on the private market exceeded the FDIC fee terms by on average 278 basis points, with considerable variation across users—varying from over 1,000 basis points above the DGP fee terms to a few basis points below. We also applied the DGP pricing rule for guaranteeing bank holding company debt to a 2-month period in 2006, before the crisis, and found that DGP pricing would have exceeded the private cost of guarantees by roughly 100 basis points. This pricing suggests that DGP would have become less attractive to participants as market conditions improved. For more detail on our analysis of the prices and terms of all of the emergency programs, please see appendix III.

---

[44]For debt issued on or after April 1, 2009, FDIC included an additional surcharge of between 10 and 50 basis points for debt with a maturity of 1 year or more. Most DGP-guaranteed debt with a maturity of 1 year or more was issued prior to April 1, 2009.

[45]We created a weighted average of 1-year CDS prices with weights based on the largest bank holding company users of DGP. Our results may not reflect the relative price of DGP for DGP participants that were not included in the weighted average.

GAO-14-18 Government Support for Bank Holding Companies

Programs Provided Support to Banking Organizations of Various Sizes and Some Programs Supported Funding Sources Used More by Larger Firms

Emergency government programs to stabilize financial markets provided funding support to bank holding companies and insured depository institutions (collectively, banking organizations) of various sizes.[46] This section also focuses on the programs that provided the most significant funding support directly to bank holding companies and their subsidiaries (listed previously in table 1). Agencies made these programs available to specific types of institutions regardless of their size, and institutions of various sizes participated in these programs. Differences in the level of program use by institutions of various sizes were driven in part by differences in how institutions funded themselves. For example, compared to smaller bank holding companies, larger bank holding companies relied to a greater extent on short-term credit markets that were the most severely disrupted during the crisis and participated more in programs intended to address disruptions in these markets. Smaller banking organizations relied more on deposits to fund their activities.

To compare the extent to which banking organizations of various sizes used emergency programs, we calculated the percentage of banking organization assets that were supported by emergency programs—either through capital injections, loans, or guarantees—at quarter-end dates for 2008 through 2012. Capital provided by emergency programs includes capital investments by Treasury under CPP and TIP. Loans provided by emergency programs include TAF, TSLF, PDCF, and CPFF loans from the Federal Reserve System. Funding guaranteed by emergency programs includes deposits guaranteed by FDIC through TAGP and debt guaranteed by FDIC through DGP. We then calculated each of these three types of liabilities as a percentage of assets for banking organizations by size for quarter-end dates from mid-2008 to the end of 2012. Finally, for each of the three types of liabilities, we decomposed average liabilities as a percentage of assets for banking organizations of different sizes into two components: (1) the rate of participation in emergency programs by banking organizations of different sizes and (2) the average liabilities as a percentage of assets for those participants.

We found that the extent to which banking organizations of different sizes used emergency programs varied over time and across programs. For

---

[46]Our analysis focuses on use of emergency programs by banking organizations. However, emergency programs also provided funding for some nonbank financial institutions, such as broker-dealers, and for some nonfinancial companies, such as McDonald's Corp. and Harley-Davidson.

example, the largest bank holding companies—those with more than $500 billion in assets as of June 30, 2013—used the programs to varying degrees but had exited most of the programs by the end of 2009. Moreover, as of December 31, 2008, average use of emergency programs generally was higher for banking organizations with $50 billion or more in assets than it was for banking organizations with less than $50 billion in assets. Total loans outstanding from Federal Reserve System programs (TAF, TSLF, PDCF, and CPFF) combined were at least 2 percent of assets on average for banking organizations with $50 billion or more in assets but less than 1 percent of assets on average for smaller banking organizations. CPP and TIP capital investments were at least 1.5 percent of assets on average for banking organizations with $50 billion or more in assets and less than 1 percent of assets on average for smaller organizations. Finally, DGP-guaranteed debt and TAGP-guaranteed deposits together were at least 6 percent of assets on average for banking organizations with $50 billion or more in assets and were less than 4 percent of assets on average for smaller banking organizations. However, by December 31, 2010, the Federal Reserve System's loan programs had closed, and differences in use of remaining programs by banking organizations of different sizes had diminished. For a more detailed discussion of our analysis of utilization of these programs by banking organizations of various sizes, see appendix IV.

Several factors influenced the extent to which eligible institutions used emergency programs. As explained above, one factor driving an institution's level of participation in a program was the extent to which it relied on the type of funding assisted by the program. In addition, market conditions and the speed with which eligible firms recovered affected the amount and duration of use of the programs by different firms. Agencies generally designed program terms and conditions to make the programs attractive only for institutions facing liquidity strains. Use of several of the programs peaked during the height of the financial crisis and fell as market conditions recovered. Federal Reserve Board officials told us that even as markets recovered, funding conditions improved for certain borrowers but not others. As a result, in PDCF, TSLF, and CPFF, several participants remained in the programs while others exited. Participants in CPP required the approval of their primary federal regulator before exiting the program. In addition, several of the programs included limits on the amount of assistance an entity could receive. Under CPP, qualified financial institutions were eligible to receive an investment of between 1 and 3 percent of their risk-weighted assets, up to a maximum of $25 billion. To prevent excessive use of CPFF that would be inconsistent with its role as a backstop, the Federal Reserve Board limited the maximum amount a single issuer could have outstanding at CPFF to the greatest amount of U.S.-dollar-denominated commercial paper the issuer had had outstanding on any day between January 1 and August 31, 2008. The Federal Reserve Board also set limits on the maximum amount that institutions could bid in each TAF and TSLF auction.[47] Finally, in some cases, institutions accepted emergency government assistance at the encouragement of their regulators. For example, several institutions accepted TARP capital investments at the encouragement of Treasury or their regulator.[48] However, participation in other programs appears to have been driven by market conditions and other factors.

The Federal Reserve Board Granted Exemptions to Allow Banks to Provide Liquidity Support to the Nonbanking Sector and for Other Purposes

During the financial crisis, the Federal Reserve Board granted a number of exemptions to requirements under Section 23A of the Federal Reserve Act for a range of purposes, such as allowing banks to provide greater liquidity support to the nonbank sector. The number of exemptions granted increased significantly during the crisis, and the majority of these exemptions were granted to U.S. bank holding companies and other firms with $500 billion or more in total assets (see fig. 2). Section 23A of the Federal Reserve Act imposes quantitative limits on certain transactions between an insured depository institution and its affiliates, prohibits banks from purchasing low-quality assets from their nonbank affiliates, and imposes collateral requirements on extensions of credit to affiliates.[49] In letters documenting its approval of exemptions to Section 23A, the Federal Reserve Board has indicated that the twin purposes of Section 23A are (1) to protect against a depository institution suffering losses in transactions with its affiliates, and (2) to limit the ability of a depository institution to transfer to its affiliates the subsidy arising from the institution's access to the federal safety net.[50] In other words, these

---

[47]In addition, TAF program terms stated that a depository institution's TAF loans outstanding with terms greater than 28 days could not exceed 75 percent of the value of collateral it had pledged to the discount window.

[48]For example, in October 2008, nine of the largest financial institutions agreed to accept TARP capital investments in part to signal the importance of the program to the stability of the financial system.

[49]Pub. L. No. 63-43, § 23A, 38 Stat. 251, 272 (12 U.S.C. § 371c).

[50]Section 23A requirements—and the associated concerns about transfer of the subsidy arising from the depository institution's access to federal safety nets—apply to depository institutions of all sizes.

restrictions are intended to protect the safety and soundness of banks and to prevent them from subsidizing the activities of nonbank affiliates by passing on any benefits they may receive through access to deposit insurance and the discount window. The Federal Reserve Act granted the Federal Reserve Board authority to exempt transactions and relationships from Section 23A restrictions if such exemptions were in the public interest and consistent with statutory purposes.[51] Prior to the Dodd-Frank Act, the Federal Reserve Board had exclusive authority to grant exemptions to Section 23A.

Figure 2: Section 23A Exemptions for Firms by Total Assets, 2000-2011

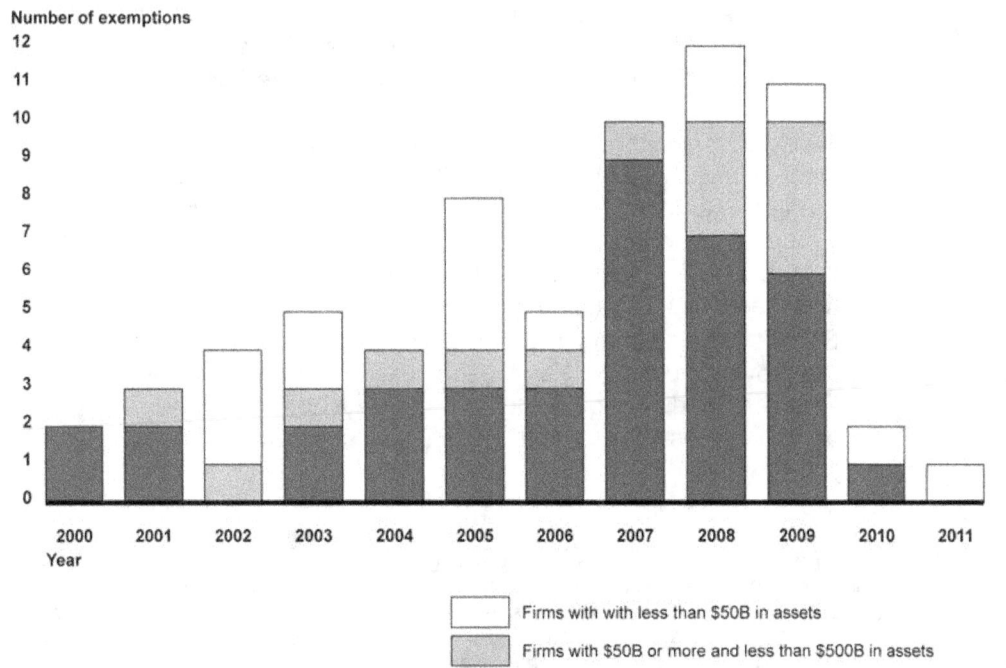

Number of exemptions

Firms with with less than $50B in assets

Firms with $50B or more and less than $500B in assets

Firms with $500B or more in assets

Source: GAO analysis of Federal Reserve Board documents.

During the financial crisis, the Federal Reserve Board granted a number of exemptions from the requirements of Section 23A, for a range of purposes that included, but were not limited to, the following:

---

[51] 12 U.S.C. § 371c(f)(2).

GAO-14-18 Government Support for Bank Holding Companies

- *Facilitating Liquidity Support for Holders of Mortgage-Related Assets.* In August 2007, the Federal Reserve Board issued three similar exemption letters granting Section 23A exemptions to three of the largest U.S. bank holding companies (Citigroup Inc., Bank of America Corporation, and JP Morgan Chase & Co.) to allow their bank subsidiaries (Citibank, N.A.; Bank of America, N.A.; and JPMorgan Chase Bank, N.A.) to engage in securities financing transactions with their affiliated broker-dealers. The purpose of these exemptions was to allow each of these banks to extend up to $25 billion of credit (using their broker-dealer affiliates as conduits) to unaffiliated market participants in need of short-term liquidity to finance their holdings of certain mortgage loans and other assets.[52] The Federal Reserve Board's letters noted that these exemptions would provide significant public benefits by allowing banks to provide a substantial amount of liquidity into the market for these mortgage-related assets.

- *Facilitating Liquidity Support for Holders of Auction-Rate Securities.* In December 2008 and January 2009, the Federal Reserve Board granted exemptions to allow four large banks (Fifth Third Bank, BB&T Company, Northern Trust Company, and Wachovia Bank, N.A.) to purchase auction-rate securities and variable rate demand notes from their securities affiliates or parent company.[53] The Federal Reserve Board's letters noted that these exemptions were intended to facilitate the provision of liquidity by these banks to customers of their affiliates that were holding illiquid auction-rate securities or variable rate demand notes.[54] The securities affiliates of banks had been active in

---

[52]The Federal Reserve Board's letters granting these exemptions noted that these banks would channel these credit transactions through their affiliated broker-dealers "for operational reasons." The transactions between each bank and broker-dealer would take the form of either reverse repurchase agreements or securities borrowing transactions and would be on the same terms as each transaction between the broker-dealer and unaffiliated market participant.

[53]As of December 31, 2008, BB&T Corp., Fifth Third Bancorp, and Northern Trust Corp had total consolidated assets of $147.5 billion, $69.5 billion, and $70.4 billion, respectively. Wachovia Corporation was the fourth largest U.S. bank holding company, with total consolidated assets of $635.5 billion. On January 1, 2009, Wells Fargo & Company completed its acquisition of Wachovia Corporation.

[54]Auction-rate securities are long-term bonds or preferred stocks whose interest rates or dividends are periodically reset through auctions. Until its collapse, the auction-rate securities market had been an important and growing source of funds for municipalities and other issuers. Variable rate demand notes are floating-rate debt instruments with a maturity of usually 20 or 30 years.

underwriting and selling auction-rate securities and when these securities became illiquid, the affiliates repurchased them from clients that sought to liquidate their positions. In this case, 23A exemptions allowed banks to provide financing for these purchases. The size of transactions permitted under these exemptions ranged from $600 million for The Northern Trust Company to approximately $7 billion for Wachovia Bank, N.A.

- *Facilitating Liquidity Support to Money Market Funds and Repurchase Agreement Markets.* In addition to exemptions granted to individual institutions, the Federal Reserve Board granted broad-based exemptions from Section 23A to enable banks to provide liquidity support to repurchase agreement markets and money market mutual funds (MMMF). First, on September 14, 2008, concurrent with the decision to expand eligible collateral types for PDCF and TSLF, the Federal Reserve Board adopted an interim final rule granting a temporary exemption to allow banks to provide their securities affiliates with short-term financing for assets that they ordinarily would have financed through the repurchase agreements markets. The purpose of this exemption was to improve the ability of broker-dealers to continue financing their securities and other assets despite the liquidity shortage in the triparty repurchase agreement market. Several days later, on September 19, the Federal Reserve Board amended Regulation W to grant a temporary exemption from Section 23A requirements for member banks' purchases of ABCP from affiliated money market funds, subject to certain conditions.[55] The purpose of this exemption was to enable banks to take full advantage of the Asset-Backed Commercial Paper Money Market Mutual Fund Liquidity Facility (AMLF), a program authorized by the Federal Reserve Board to provide loans to banks to fund the purchase of ABCP from MMMFs.

- *Facilitating Acquisitions of Failing Firms.* The Federal Reserve Board also granted Section 23A exemptions in connection with its efforts to facilitate private acquisitions of firms whose failure could have destabilized financial markets. Such acquisitions included JP Morgan Chase & Co.'s acquisition of Bear Stearns and Wells Fargo & Company's acquisition of Wachovia Corporation. JP Morgan Chase &

---

[55]*Transactions Between Member Banks and Their Affiliates: Exemption for Certain Purchases of Asset-Backed Commercial Paper by a Member Bank from an Affiliate,* 73 Fed. Reg. 55708 (Sept. 26, 2008) (amending 12 C.F.R. § 223.42 and adding § 223.56).

Co. received exemptions that allowed JP Morgan Chase Bank, N.A. to, among other things, extend credit to, and issue guarantees on behalf of, former Bear Stearns entities and to purchase a derivatives portfolio valued at approximately $44 billion from Bear Stearns. In November 2008, the Federal Reserve Board granted an exemption to allow Wells Fargo Bank, N.A., to extend up to $17 billion in credit to Wachovia Bank, N.A. to assist it in meeting its short-term funding obligations until the merger was completed.

For many of these cases, the Federal Reserve Board granted an exemption to help facilitate liquidity support to nonbank entities as part of its actions to reduce systemic risk and promote financial stability. In granting exemptions, the Federal Reserve Board imposed conditions that were intended to mitigate risks to the bank that would be providing credit, purchasing assets, or engaging in other transactions with affiliates.[56] However, one expert has raised concerns that such conditions might not offer sufficient protection for an insured depository institution during crisis conditions and that these exemptions in aggregate resulted in a large-scale transfer of safety net benefits created for banks to the nonbank, or "shadow banking," system.[57] As discussed in the next section of this report, the Dodd-Frank Act made changes to Section 23A of the Federal Reserve Act.

---

[56]Section 23B of the Federal Reserve Act generally requires that certain transactions between a bank and its affiliates occur on market terms—that is, on terms and under circumstances that are substantially the same, or at least as favorable to the bank, as those prevailing at the time for comparable transactions with unaffiliated companies. 12 U.S.C. § 371c-1(a)(1)(A). Section 23B applies to any transaction by a bank with a third party if an affiliate has a financial interest in the third party or if an affiliate is a participant in the transaction. *Id.* at (a)(2)(E).

[57]See Saule T. Omarova, "From Gramm-Leach-Bliley to Dodd-Frank: The Unfulfilled Promise of Section 23A of the Federal Reserve Act," *North Carolina Law Review,* Vol. 89, pgs. 1684-1769. The shadow banking system refers to a web of financial institutions that channel funds from savers to borrowers through a range of securitization and secured funding techniques. Unlike traditional banks, shadow banking institutions lack explicit access to the federal safety nets, such as the discount window and deposit insurance.

Some Large Bank Holding Companies Benefited from Individual Institution Assistance or Regulatory Relief

In addition to introducing emergency programs with broad-based eligibility, federal government agencies took special actions with respect to individual financial institutions on several occasions in 2008 and 2009. While these actions were intended to benefit a range of market participants and the broader financial system, some large U.S. bank holding companies received substantial direct benefits from these actions. Such actions included (1) assistance from multiple agencies to rescue or facilitate the acquisition of troubled firms whose failures posed significant risks to the financial system, and (2) the Federal Reserve Board granting bank holding company status to several nonbank financial companies and providing liquidity support to the London broker-dealers of a few of the largest bank holding companies.

Individual Institution Assistance

On several occasions in 2008 and early 2009, the federal government provided extraordinary support to or facilitated the acquisition of large financial institutions, which benefitted recipients of this assistance and other market participants, such as firms that had large risk exposures to these institutions.

- *Assistance to Facilitate JP Morgan's Acquisition of Bear Stearns.* In 2008, the Federal Reserve Board authorized emergency assistance to avert the failure of Bear Stearns Companies, Inc. (Bear Stearns) and facilitate the acquisition of the firm by JP Morgan Chase & Co.[58] On Friday, March 14, 2008, the Federal Reserve Board voted to authorize FRBNY to provide a $12.9 billion loan to Bear Stearns to enable the firm to avoid bankruptcy and to provide time for potential acquirers, including JP Morgan Chase & Co, to assess its financial condition. On Sunday, March 16, 2008, the Federal Reserve Board announced that FRBNY would lend up to $30 billion against certain Bear Stearns assets to facilitate JP Morgan Chase & Co's acquisition of Bear Stearns. During the following week, the terms of this assistance were renegotiated, resulting in the creation of a new lending structure under which a $28.82 billion FRBNY senior loan and a $1.15 billion JP Morgan Chase & Co subordinated loan funded the purchase of certain Bear Stearns's assets. FRBNY also provided certain regulatory exemptions to JP Morgan Chase & Co. in connection with its agreement to acquire Bear Stearns. For example, the Federal

---

[58]Bear Stearns was one of the largest primary dealers and engaged in a broad range of activities, including investment banking, securities and derivatives trading, brokerage services, and origination and securitization of mortgage loans.

Reserve Board granted an 18-month exemption to allow JP Morgan Chase & Co to exclude certain Bear Stearns assets from its risk-weighted assets for purposes of applying risk-based capital requirements.

- *Assistance to Government-Sponsored Enterprises.* Extraordinary government support to Fannie Mae and Freddie Mac helped to stabilize mortgage markets and the broader financial markets and provided specific benefits to bank holding companies and other firms that likely would have incurred losses if the federal government had allowed these government-sponsored enterprises to fail. On September 6, 2008, the Federal Housing Finance Agency placed Fannie Mae and Freddie Mac into conservatorship out of concern that their deteriorating financial condition threatened their safety and soundness and their ability to fulfill their public mission.[59] Treasury's investments in Fannie Mae and Freddie Mac under the Senior Preferred Stock Purchase Agreements program represent the federal government's single largest risk exposure remaining from its emergency actions to assist the financial sector.[60] As of June 30, 2013, cumulative cash draws by the GSEs under this program totaled $187.4 billion and cumulative dividends paid by the GSEs to Treasury totaled $131.6 billion.

- *Assistance to AIG.* Federal government actions to prevent the failure of AIG benefitted AIG and its counterparties—which included some of the largest U.S. and foreign financial institutions—and were intended to benefit the broader financial system.[61] In September 2008, the Federal Reserve Board and Treasury determined that market events could have caused AIG to fail, which would have posed systemic risk to financial markets. The Federal Reserve Board and Treasury collaborated to make available up to $182.3 billion in assistance to

---

[59]The Housing and Economic Recovery Act of 2008, Pub. L. No. 110-289, 122 Stat. 2654, established the Federal Housing Finance Agency, which was authorized to be appointed conservator for the government-sponsored enterprises. §§ 1101, 1145, 122 Stat. at 2661, 2734.

[60]Under the Senior Preferred Stock Purchase Agreements program, Treasury has made funding advances to Fannie Mae and Freddie Mac to ensure that they have sufficient assets to support their liabilities.

[61]AIG is a multinational insurer that was also a significant participant in the financial derivatives market.

AIG. This assistance, which began with a revolving credit facility of up to $85 billion from FRBNY, was provided in several stages and was restructured over time.[62] In November 2008, the Federal Reserve Board authorized the creation of two special-purpose vehicles—Maiden Lane II LLC and Maiden Lane III LLC—to purchase certain AIG-related assets. Maiden Lane II was created to alleviate capital and liquidity pressures arising from a securities lending portfolio operated by certain AIG subsidiaries by purchasing residential MBS held in this portfolio. Maiden Lane III helped to fund the purchase of collateralized debt obligations from AIG counterparties that had purchased CDS from AIG to protect the value of those assets. AIG repaid all loans and capital investments it received from government entities during the crisis. In December 2012, Treasury sold its remaining investments in AIG, resulting in a total positive return of $22.7 billion for Treasury and FRBNY.

- *Extraordinary Assistance to Citigroup.* On November 23, 2008, Treasury, the Federal Reserve Board, and FDIC announced a package of additional assistance to Citigroup Inc. (Citigroup) that included $20 billion of capital from TIP and a loss-sharing agreement with the government entities that was intended to assure market participants that Citigroup would not fail in the event of larger-than-expected losses on certain of its assets. As discussed in our April 2010 report on Treasury's use of the systemic risk determination, Treasury, FDIC, and the Federal Reserve Board said they provided emergency assistance to Citigroup because they were concerned that a failure of a firm of Citigroup's size and interconnectedness would have systemic implications.[63] As of September 30, 2008, Citigroup was the second largest banking organization in the United States, with total consolidated assets of approximately $2 trillion. In June 2009, Treasury entered into an agreement to exchange the $25 billion in Citigroup preferred shares purchased in its initial CPP investment for Citigroup common shares to help improve Citigroup's capital position.[64] In December 2009, Citigroup repaid the $20 billion TIP

---

[62]For more information about the federal government's actions to assist AIG and the restructuring and repayment of this assistance over time, see GAO, *Troubled Asset Relief Program: Government's Exposure to AIG Lessens as Equity Investments are Sold,* GAO-12-574 (Washington, D.C.: May 7, 2012).

[63]See GAO-10-100.

[64]In December 2010, Treasury sold its remaining shares of Citigroup common stock.

investment. On December 23, 2009, Citigroup announced that it had entered into an agreement with FDIC, FRBNY, and Treasury to terminate the loss- sharing agreement. As part of the termination agreement, Citigroup agreed to pay a $50 million termination fee to FRBNY.

- *Extraordinary Assistance to Bank of America.* On January 16, 2009, Treasury, the Federal Reserve Board, and FDIC announced a similar package of assistance to Bank of America Corporation (Bank of America). The additional assistance included capital through TIP and a loss-sharing agreement that was similar to the one executed for Citigroup. While Bank of America received $20 billion in capital through TIP, the government entities never finalized the announced loss-sharing agreement with Bank of America. In September 2009, the agencies agreed to terminate the loss-sharing agreement with Bank of America. As part of the agreement to terminate the agreement-in-principle, Bank of America paid fees of $276 million to Treasury, $57 million to the Federal Reserve Board, and $92 million to FDIC. Bank of America repaid its $20 billion TIP investment in December 2009.

Bank Holding Company Status and Liquidity Support for London Subsidiaries

In late 2008, at the height of the financial crisis, the Federal Reserve Board approved applications by several large nonbank financial firms to convert to bank holding company status. Becoming bank holding companies provided these firms with greater access to emergency government funding support, while subjecting them to oversight by the Federal Reserve System and other requirements under the Bank Holding Company Act.[65] Eligibility for TARP capital investments under CPP and debt guarantees through TLGP were generally restricted to depository institutions and their holding companies, and several large firms that became bank holding companies in late 2008 subsequently participated in one or both of these programs. Among the largest firms converting to bank holding companies during the crisis were two investment banks (Goldman Sachs Group, Inc. and Morgan Stanley), two companies that were large providers of credit card products and other services (American Express Company and Discover Financial Services), and two other financial firms (CIT Group Inc. and GMAC LLC). In many cases, obtaining bank holding company status involved firms converting an industrial loan

---

[65]Pub. L. No. 84-511, 70 Stat. 133 (codified at 12 U.S.C. §§ 1841-1852).

corporation (ILC) into a bank.[66] Federal Reserve Board officials noted that these firms already had access to the discount window through their ILCs and converting these ILCs to banks did not change their access to the discount window, but their access to discount window liquidity was limited by the amount of assets these subsidiaries—first as ILCs and later as banks—could pledge to the discount window as collateral. According to Federal Reserve Board documents, deposits held by these firms were a small fraction of their total consolidated assets at the time they became bank holding companies. While bank holding companies are subject to restrictions on nonbanking activities under the Bank Holding Company Act, Federal Reserve Board orders approving bank holding company applications described nonbanking activities of the companies that were permissible under the act and noted that the act provides each newly formed bank holding company 2 years to conform its existing nonbanking investments and activities to the act's requirements.

On September 21, 2008, the Federal Reserve Board announced that FRBNY would extend credit—on terms similar to those applicable for PDCF loans—to the U.S. and London broker-dealer subsidiaries of Goldman Sachs Group, Inc., Morgan Stanley, and Merrill Lynch & Co. to provide support to these subsidiaries as they became part of bank holding companies that would be regulated by the Federal Reserve System.[67] On November 23, 2008, in connection with other actions taken by Treasury, FDIC, and the Federal Reserve Board to assist Citigroup, the Federal Reserve Board authorized FRBNY to extend credit to the London-based

---

[66]For various reasons, the Bank Holding Company Act exempts from regulation certain companies that own depository institutions; these subsidiaries are not defined as banks for purposes of the act and thus the companies that own them are not considered bank holding companies and are not required to comply with the act's restrictions. 12 U.S.C. § 1841(c)(2). One type of these companies is the ILC. *Id.* at § 1841(c)(2)(H). ILCs are limited-service financial institutions that make loans and raise funds by selling certificates called "investment shares" and by accepting deposits. ILCs are distinguished from finance companies because ILCs accept deposits in addition to making consumer loans. ILCs also differ from commercial banks because most ILCs do not offer demand deposit (checking) accounts. For more information about ILCs and other exempt companies, see GAO, *Bank Holding Company Act: Characteristics and Regulation of Exempt Institutions and the Implications of Removing the Exemptions*, GAO-12-160 (Washington, D.C.: Jan. 19, 2012).

[67]On that same day, Bank of America had agreed to acquire Merrill Lynch & Co., which would become part of a bank holding company pending completion of its merger with Bank of America, a bank holding company supervised by the Federal Reserve System upon completion of the acquisition.

broker-dealer of Citigroup on terms similar to those applicable to PDCF loans.

Dodd-Frank Aims to Restrict Future Government Support, but Implementation Is Incomplete and Effectiveness Remains Uncertain

Enacted in July 2010, the Dodd-Frank Act contains provisions intended to modify the scope of federal safety nets for financial firms, place limits on agency authorities to provide emergency assistance, and strengthen regulatory oversight of the largest firms, among other things.[68] FDIC and the Federal Reserve Board have finalized certain changes to traditional safety nets for insured banks, but impacts of the act's provisions to limit the scope of financial transactions that benefit from these safety nets will depend on how they are implemented. The act also prohibits regulators' use of emergency authorities to rescue an individual institution and places other restrictions on these authorities. For example, the act effectively removes FDIC's authority to provide assistance to a single, specific failing bank outside of receivership and grants FDIC new authority to resolve a large failing institution outside of bankruptcy.[69] FDIC has made progress toward implementing its new resolution authority and continues to work to address potential obstacles to the viability of its resolution process as an alternative to bankruptcy, such as challenges that could arise when resolving more than one large institution concurrently. The act also places new restrictions and requirements on the Federal Reserve Board's emergency lending authority. However, the Federal Reserve Board has not yet completed its process for drafting policies and procedures required by the act to implement these changes or set timeframes for doing so. Finalizing such procedures would help ensure that any future use of this authority complies with Dodd-Frank Act requirements. Finally, the Federal Reserve Board has made progress towards implementing certain enhanced regulatory standards that are intended to reduce the risks that the largest financial institutions pose to the financial system.

---

[68]See generally Pub. L. No. 111-203, 124 Stat. 1376 (2010).

[69]§§ 204, 210, 124 Stat. at 1454-56, 1460.

Agencies Have Finalized Changes to Traditional Safety Nets, but Have Not Fully Implemented Provisions to Limit the Scope of Transactions That Have Access

The Dodd-Frank Act instituted a series of reforms related to the traditional safety nets for insured banks, including changes to deposit insurance and discount window reporting requirements. In addition, the act contains provisions intended to limit the scope of financial transactions that benefit from access to these traditional safety nets. These provisions include revisions to the Federal Reserve Board's authority to permit certain transactions between banks and their affiliates under Section 23A of the Federal Reserve Act, restrictions on the ability of bank holding companies to engage in proprietary trading; and restrictions on the ability of insured banks to engage in certain derivatives transactions.

Deposit Insurance

FDIC has implemented Dodd-Frank Act provisions that increased the deposit insurance limit and required FDIC to change the calculation for premiums paid by insured depository institutions. Section 335 of the Dodd-Frank Act permanently raised the standard maximum deposit insurance amount from $100,000 to $250,000 for individual deposit accounts, as previously discussed.[70] FDIC issued and made effective a final rule instituting the increase in August 2010 and required insured depository institutions to comply by January 2011.[71] Section 343 of the act provided temporary unlimited deposit insurance coverage for certain uninsured deposits from December 2010 through December 2012.[72] This coverage expired on December 31, 2012, and transaction accounts can now only be insured to the $250,000 ceiling.[73] Section 331 of the Dodd-Frank Act required FDIC to amend its regulation and modify the definition of an insured depository institution's assessment base, which can affect the amount of deposit insurance assessment the institution pays into the deposit insurance fund. Under the Dodd-Frank Act, the assessment base changed from total domestic deposits to average consolidated total assets minus average tangible equity (with some possible exceptions).[74] FDIC issued a final rule changing the assessment base in February 2011, and the rule became effective in April 2011.[75] According to FDIC, the

---

[70]§335, 124 Stat. at 1540.

[71]*Deposit Insurance Regulations; Permanent Increase in Standard Coverage Amount*, 75 Fed. Reg. 49363 (Aug. 13, 2010).

[72] §343(a), 124 Stat. at 1544.

[73]*Id.*

[74]§331(b), 124 Stat. at 1538.

[75]*Assessments, Large Bank Pricing*, 76 Fed. Reg. 10672 (Feb. 25, 2011).

change in the assessment base calculation shifted some of the overall assessment burden from community banks to larger institutions that rely less on domestic deposits for their funding than smaller institutions, but without affecting the overall amount of assessment revenue collected.[76] In the quarter after the rule became effective, those banks with less than $10 billion in assets saw a 33 percent drop in their assessments (from about $1 billion to about $700 million), while those banks with over $10 billion in assets saw a 17 percent rise in their assessments (from about $2.4 billion to about $2.8 billion).

Discount Window Reporting Requirements

The Dodd-Frank Act made changes to the Federal Reserve Board's reporting requirements to increase the transparency for discount window transactions. During and after the crisis, some members of Congress and others expressed concern that certain details of the Federal Reserve System's discount window and emergency lending activities, including the names of borrowers receiving loans, were kept confidential. Section 1103 of the Dodd-Frank Act requires the Federal Reserve Board to disclose transaction-level details for discount window loans and open market transactions on a quarterly basis after a 2-year delay.[77] The Dodd-Frank Act established similar reporting requirements for the Federal Reserve Board's Section 13(3) authority, as discussed later. No rulemaking was required, and the Federal Reserve Board began to post the data publicly on its website in September 2012. The first set of releases covered loans made between July and September 2010, and data for subsequent periods are being published quarterly with a 2-year lag. The Dodd-Frank Act also grants GAO authority to audit certain aspects of discount window transactions occurring after July 21, 2010.

Section 23A

The Dodd-Frank Act made numerous changes to Section 23A of the Federal Reserve Act that both significantly expanded the scope of activities covered by Section 23A's restrictions and created new requirements for participation by FDIC and the OCC in granting

---

[76]For more information on this rule, see GAO, *Dodd-Frank Act Regulations: Implementation Could Benefit from Additional Analyses and Coordination,* GAO-12-151 (Washington, D.C.: Nov. 10, 2011).

[77]§ 1103(b), 124 Stat. at 2118.

exceptions.[78] As previously discussed, the Federal Reserve Board granted a number of exemptions to Section 23A during the crisis. Some observers have raised concerns that these exemptions in aggregate resulted in a large scale transfer of federal safety net benefits to the nonbank, or "shadow banking," system. The changes listed below, with the exception of changes related to investments in private funds, did not require rulemakings and became effective on July 21, 2012.

- The Dodd-Frank Act gave FDIC and OCC, jointly with the Federal Reserve Board, the authority to grant Section 23A exemptions by order for institutions they supervise. The Dodd-Frank Act requires the regulators to notify FDIC of any proposed exemption and give FDIC 60 days to object in writing, should FDIC determine the proposed exemption constitutes an unacceptable risk to the deposit insurance fund.[79] The Federal Reserve retains the authority to grant exemptions by regulation.

- The Dodd-Frank Act expanded the scope of activities that are covered by Section 23A by amending the definition of covered transactions to include derivatives transactions with affiliates and transactions with affiliates that involve securities lending and borrowing that may cause a bank to face credit exposure to an affiliate.[80] The Dodd-Frank Act also removed the exception from the 10 percent quantitative limit for certain covered transactions between a bank and its financial subsidiary and extended section 23A and 23B to cover permitted investments in certain private funds.

- The Dodd-Frank Act changed the collateral requirements for 23A transactions by requiring banks to maintain the correct level of

---

[78]Section 23A of the Federal Reserve Act restricts the ability of banks to provide funding to their nonbank affiliates above a certain limit, and imposes collateral and other requirements for those transactions. The goals of Section 23A are to protect federally insured banks from too much exposure to riskier nonbank affiliates and to prevent the transfer of the federal subsidy to nondepository institutions.

[79]§ 608(a), 124 Stat. at 1609-10.

[80]§ 608(a)(1)(A), 124 Stat. at 1608. Section 23B generally requires that certain transactions between a bank and its affiliates occur on market terms; that is, on terms and under circumstances that are substantially the same, or at least as favorable to the bank, as those prevailing at the time for comparable transactions with unaffiliated companies. Section 23B applies to any transaction by a bank with a third party if an affiliate has a financial interest in the third party or if an affiliate is a participant in the transaction.

collateral at all times for covered transactions subject to collateralization.[81] Previously, banks only had to post collateral at the time of entrance into the covered transaction. This change was designed to strengthen the protection granted to banks extending credit to their affiliates by ensuring that the collateral remains correctly valued and simultaneously shields the bank's interest from fluctuations in market prices of collateralized assets.

As of October 2013, the Federal Reserve Board has granted only two exemptions since the enactment of the Dodd-Frank Act, according to available information on its website. How the Federal Reserve Board, FDIC, and OCC might respond to requests for exemptions in the future is uncertain. Representatives from one large bank told us that their primary regulator advised them that that because of FDIC's required approval, they should not expect exemptions to be available going forward. However, one academic has expressed concern about how exemptions might be applied under different circumstances, such as in periods of economic stress.

Proprietary Trading (Volcker Rule)

Agencies have not yet issued final rules to implement the Dodd-Frank Act's restrictions on proprietary trading—trading activities conducted by banking entities for their own account as opposed to those of their clients. A number of market participants and researchers with whom we spoke maintain that the ability of banking entities to use federally insured deposits to seek profits for their own account provides incentives for them to take on excessive risk. To address these concerns, Section 619 of the Dodd-Frank Act (also known as the Volcker Rule) generally prohibits proprietary trading by insured depository institutions and their affiliates and places restrictions on sponsorship or investment in hedge and private equity funds. An FSOC study noted that implementing the act's restrictions on proprietary trading will be challenging because certain trading activities exempted from the act's restrictions may appear very similar to proprietary trading activities that the act seeks to restrict. While

---

[81]§ 608(a)(2), 124 Stat. at 1608.

regulators issued proposed rules in November 2011 and February 2012, no final or interim final rules have been issued.[82]

Restrictions on Some Derivatives Transactions

Section 716 of the Dodd-Frank Act requires banks that are registered dealers of derivatives known as swaps to transfer certain swap activities to nonbank affiliates, or lose access to deposit insurance and the Federal Reserve System liquidity provided through the discount window for certain activities taken in connection with the swap entity's swap business.[83] Section 716's prohibition on federal assistance to swaps entities became effective in July 2013, but the law allowed for an initial 2-year extension as well as an additional 1-year extension. Several banks applied for and were granted 2-year extensions by the Federal Reserve Board and OCC, and those financial institutions now have until July 2015 to comply, with the additional option of applying for another 1-year exemption.

Dodd-Frank Restricts Certain FDIC Authorities but Provides New Resolution Authority

The Dodd-Frank Act restricts emergency authorities used by financial regulators during the most recent financial crisis, such as FDIC's open bank assistance authority; provides FDIC with new resolution authority to resolve a large, complex failing firm in a manner that limits the disruption to the financial system; and establishes a requirement for certain firms to develop and submit to regulators resolution plans (known as living wills) for their resolution under bankruptcy.

Open Bank Assistance

The Dodd-Frank Act restricts FDIC's authority to provide open bank assistance to an individual failing bank outside of receivership and replaces it with a new authority, subject to certain restrictions and a joint

---

[82]*Prohibitions and Restrictions on Proprietary Trading and Certain Interests in, and Relationships With, Hedge Funds and Covered Funds; Proposed Rule*, 77 Fed. Reg. 8332 (Feb. 14, 2012); *Prohibitions and Restrictions on Proprietary Trading and Certain Interests in, and Relationships With, Hedge Funds and Private Equity Funds; Proposed Rule*, 76 Fed. Reg. 68846 (Nov. 7, 2011).

[83]§ 716(a), 124 Stat. at 1648. A swap is a type of derivative that involves an ongoing exchange of one or more assets, liabilities, or payments for a specified period. Financial and nonfinancial firms use swaps and other derivatives to hedge risk, or speculate, or for other purposes. Swaps include interest rate swaps, commodity-based swaps, and broad-based credit default swaps. Security-based swaps include single-name and narrow-based credit default swaps and equity-based swaps. Certain insured depository institutions are excluded from the definition of "swaps entity" and are therefore exempt from Section 716 restrictions. § 716(b)(2)(B).

resolution of congressional approval, to create a debt-guarantee program with broad-based eligibility.[84] Previously, FDIC could provide open bank assistance upon a joint determination by FDIC, the Federal Reserve Board, and the Secretary of the Treasury that compliance with certain cost limitations would result in serious adverse effects on economic conditions or financial stability and that such assistance could mitigate these systemic effects.[85] Sections 1104 through 1106 of the Dodd-Frank Act provide permanent authority for FDIC to establish a widely available program to guarantee certain debt obligations of solvent insured depository institutions or solvent bank holding companies during times of severe economic distress, upon a liquidity event finding. In addition, institutions would have to pay fees for these guarantees as they did under TLGP during the crisis.[86] In order for FDIC to exercise the authority, the Dodd-Frank Act requires the Secretary of the Treasury (in consultation with the President) to determine the maximum amount of debt outstanding that FDIC can guarantee, and the guarantee authority requires congressional approval.[87] Furthermore, the Dodd-Frank Act amendments to the Federal Deposit Insurance Act that provided for temporary unlimited deposit insurance for noninterest-bearing transaction accounts were repealed as of January 1, 2013. The FDIC may not rely on this authority or its former systemic risk exception authority to provide unlimited deposit insurance for transaction accounts in a future crisis.

Resolution Authority

The Dodd-Frank Act includes two key reforms intended to facilitate the orderly resolution of a large failing firm without a taxpayer-funded rescue: (1) the Orderly Liquidation Authority (OLA), through which FDIC can liquidate large financial firms outside of the bankruptcy process; and (2) requirements for bank holding companies with $50 billion or more in assets and nonbank financial companies designated by FSOC to

---

[84]§§ 1105(a), 1106(b), 124 Stat. at 2121, 2125.

[85]For more information about the systemic risk exception, see GAO, *Federal Deposit Insurance Act: Regulators' Use of Systemic Risk Exception Raises Moral Hazard Concerns and Opportunities Exist to Clarify the Provision*, GAO-10-100 (Washington, D.C.: Apr. 15, 2010). A systemic risk determination exempts FDIC from the Federal Deposit Insurance Act's least-cost rule, which requires FDIC to use the least costly method when assisting an insured institution and prohibits FDIC from increasing losses to the Deposit Insurance Fund by protecting creditors and uninsured depositors of an insured institution.

[86]§ 1105(e), 124 Stat. at 2124.

[87]§ 1105(c)-(d), 124 Stat. at 2121-2122.

formulate and submit to regulators resolution plans (or "living wills") that detail how the companies could be resolved in bankruptcy in the event of a material financial distress or failure.[88]

OLA gives FDIC the authority, subject to certain constraints, to liquidate large financial firms, including nonbanks, outside of the bankruptcy process.[89] This authority allows for FDIC to be appointed receiver for a financial firm if the Secretary of the Treasury determines that the firm's failure and its resolution under applicable federal or state law, including bankruptcy, would have serious adverse effects on U.S. financial stability and no viable private sector alternative is available to prevent the default of the financial company.[90] While the Dodd-Frank Act does not specify how FDIC must exercise its OLA resolution authority and while a number of approaches have been considered, FDIC's preferred approach to resolving a firm under OLA is referred to as Single Point-of-Entry (SPOE). Under the SPOE approach, FDIC would be appointed receiver of a top-tier U.S. parent holding company of the financial group determined to be in default or in danger of default following the completion of the appointment process set forth under the Dodd-Frank Act. Immediately after placing the parent holding company into receivership, FDIC would

---

[88]During the financial crisis, several large financial institutions became insolvent and filed for bankruptcy when no private-sector solution was found. For example, Lehman Brothers filed for Chapter 11 bankruptcy on the morning of September 15, 2008. Lehman had $639 billion in total assets and $613 billion in total liabilities as of May 31, 2008. The bankruptcy proceedings highlighted inconsistencies in laws and regulations across countries and limitations on the ability of countries to coordinate effectively during the reorganization or liquidation of international financial institutions. Bankruptcy is a federal court procedure conducted under rules and requirements of the U.S. Bankruptcy Code. The goal of bankruptcy is to give individuals and businesses a "fresh start" from burdensome debts by eliminating or restructuring debts they cannot repay and help creditors receive some payment in an equitable manner through liquidation or reorganization of the debtor.

[89]§ 204, 124 Stat. at 1454-1456.

[90]§ 204(b), 124 Stat. at 1455. The factors to be addressed are set forth in Section 203(b) of the Dodd-Frank Act. § 203(b), 124 Stat. at 1451. Before the Secretary of the Treasury, in consultation with the President, makes a decision to appoint FDIC as receiver of a covered financial company, at least two-thirds of those serving on the Board of Governors of the Federal Reserve System and at least two-thirds of those serving on the Board of Directors of FDIC must vote to make a written recommendation to the Secretary of the Treasury to appoint FDIC as receiver. § 203(a), 124 Stat. at 1450. In the case of a broker-dealer, the recommendation must come from the Federal Reserve Board and the Securities and Exchange Commission, in consultation with FDIC, and in the case of an insurance company from the Federal Reserve Board and the Director of the Federal Insurance Office, in consultation with FDIC.

transfer some assets (primarily the equity and investments in subsidiaries) from the receivership estate to a bridge financial holding company. By taking control of the firm at the holding company level, this approach is intended to allow subsidiaries (domestic and foreign) carrying out critical services to remain open and operating. One key factor for the success of the SPOE approach is ensuring that the holding company builds up sufficient loss-absorbing capacity to enable it to recapitalize its subsidiaries, if necessary.

In a SPOE resolution, at the parent holding company level, shareholders would be wiped out, and unsecured debt holders would have their claims written down to reflect any losses that shareholders cannot cover. Under the Dodd-Frank Act, officers and directors responsible for the failure cannot be retained.[91] FDIC expects the well-capitalized bridge financial company and its subsidiaries to borrow in the private markets and from customary sources of liquidity. The new resolution authority under the Dodd- Frank Act provides a back-up source for liquidity support, the Orderly Liquidation Fund, which could provide liquidity support to the bridge financial company if customary sources of liquidity are unavailable.[92] The law requires FDIC to recover any losses arising from a resolution by assessing bank holding companies with $50 billion or more in consolidated assets, nonbank financial holding companies designated for supervision by the Federal Reserve System, and other financial companies with $50 billion or more in consolidated assets.[93]

Progress has been made to implement the reforms related to resolving large, complex financial institutions. FDIC has largely completed the core rulemakings necessary to carry out its systemic resolution responsibilities. For example, FDIC approved a final rule implementing OLA that addressed the priority of claims and the treatment of similarly situated creditors.[94] The FDIC plans to seek public comment on its resolution strategy by the end of 2013. In addition, FDIC has worked with other financial regulatory agencies, both domestic and foreign, to make

---

[91]§ 204(a)(2), 124 Stat. at 1454.

[92]§ 210(n), 124 Stat. at 1506.

[93]§ 210(o)(1), 124 Stat. at 1509.

[94]*Certain Orderly Liquidation Authority Provisions under Title II of the Dodd-Frank Wall Street Reform and Consumer Protection Act*, 76 Fed. Reg. 41626 (July 15, 2011).

extensive preparations and to conduct planning exercises in order to be as prepared as possible to successfully resolve a firm whose failure could threaten the stability of the financial system.

Although progress has been made, FDIC and others have acknowledged that OLA is new and untested, and several challenges to its effectiveness remain. For example, FDIC could face difficulties in effectively managing the failure of one or more large bank holding companies or credibly imposing losses on the creditors of those holding companies. These challenges include the following:

- *Financial stability concerns.* FDIC may find it difficult to impose losses on all creditors of failing financial institutions because of concerns about financial stability. FDIC could in principle transfer certain bank holding company liabilities to a bridge holding company in order to protect those creditors. This concern has been subject to debate. For example, a report by the Bipartisan Policy Center, a think-tank, emphasized the importance of protecting short-term creditors of systemically important firms, while an industry association report emphasized the importance of imposing losses on short-term creditors in order to maintain market discipline.[95] While the Dodd-Frank Act allows FDIC to treat similarly situated creditors differently, it places restrictions on FDIC's ability to do so. Any transfer of liabilities from the receivership to the bridge financial company that has a disparate impact upon similarly situated creditors will only be made if such a transfer will maximize the return to those creditors left in the receivership and if such action is necessary to initiate and continue operations essential to the bridge financial company.[96]

- *Global cooperation.* Some experts have questioned how FDIC would handle issues related to the non-U.S. subsidiaries of a failed firm. For example, if a global U.S. firm were at risk of being placed in receivership under OLA, foreign regulators might act to ring-fence assets of a non-U.S. subsidiary to prevent these assets from being transferred abroad where they would not be available to protect

---

[95]Bipartisan Policy Center, *Too Big to Fail: The Path to a Solution* (Washington, D.C.: May 2013), The Clearing House, *Report on the Orderly Liquidation Authority Resolution Symposium and Simulation* (New York, N.Y.: January 2013).

[96]*See* Pub. L. No. 111-203, § 210(h)(5)(E), 124 Stat. 1376, 1499 (2010); 12 U.S.C. § 5390(b)(4)(A)(ii); 12 CFR 380.27.

counterparties in their jurisdiction. Such a development could increase financial instability by reducing the assets available to a U.S. firm to satisfy creditors' claims. Because SPOE involves losses borne only by holding company creditors, some observers have suggested this approach would avoid potential challenges associated with the failure of foreign subsidiaries or actions of foreign regulators to ring-fence the assets of a subsidiary. For example, if subsidiary liabilities were guaranteed under SPOE, foreign regulators would not need to ring-fence foreign subsidiaries in order to protect foreign customers or creditors.

- *Multiple, simultaneous insolvencies.* Experts have questioned whether FDIC has sufficient capacity to use OLA to handle multiple failures of systemically important firms and thus prevent further systemic disruption. In addition, FDIC may find it more difficult to impose losses on creditors when multiple large institutions are failing at once, which could reduce the credibility of OLA. According to a survey of investors, few respondents believed that FDIC could effectively use OLA to handle the resolution of multiple firms simultaneously.[97]

Living Wills

Title I of the Dodd-Frank Act requires bank holding companies with $50 billion or more in consolidated assets and nonbank financial companies designated by FSOC to formulate and submit to FDIC, the Federal Reserve Board, and FSOC resolution plans (or "living wills") that detail how the companies could be resolved in the event of material financial distress or failure.[98] The Federal Reserve Board and FDIC finalized rules relating to resolution plans, and the large financial institutions that were the first firms required to prepare such plans submitted these to regulators as expected in July 2012.[99] Regulators reviewed these initial plans and developed guidance on what information should be included in 2013 resolution plan submissions.[100]

---

[97]Barclays, *TBTF: The $83bn Question* (New York, N.Y.: July 1, 2013).

[98]§ 165(d)(1), 124 Stat. at 1426.

[99]*Living Wills Required*, 76 Fed. Reg. 67323 (Nov. 1, 2011).

[100]In October 2013, the Federal Reserve Board and FDIC released the public sections of filed annual resolution plans for 11 firms. Federal Reserve Board and FDIC, Agencies Release Public Sections of the Second Submission of Resolution Plans for 11 Institutions, accessed on November 7, 2013, http://www.federalreserve.gov/newsevents/press/bcreg/20131003a.htm

Experts have expressed mixed views on the usefulness of the living wills. Some experts have noted that resolution plans may provide regulators with critical information about a firm's organizational structure that could aid the resolution process or motivate complex firms to simplify their structures, and this simplification could help facilitate resolution. However, other experts have told us that resolution plans may provide limited benefits in simplifying firm structures, in part because tax, jurisdictional, and other considerations may outweigh the benefits of simplification. Furthermore, some experts commented that although resolution plans may assist regulators in gaining a better understanding of the structures and activities of complex financial firms, the plans may not be useful guides during an actual liquidation—in part because the plans could become outdated or because the plans may not be helpful during a crisis.

Dodd-Frank Restricts Emergency Lending Authority, but the Federal Reserve Board Has Not Completed its Process for Drafting Required Procedures

The Dodd-Frank Act creates new restrictions and requirements associated with the Federal Reserve Board's Section 13(3) authority.[101] Generally, the act prohibits use of Section 13(3) authority to assist an individual institution (as the Federal Reserve Board did with Bear Stearns and AIG). While the act continues to allow the Federal Reserve Board to use 13(3) authority to authorize programs with broad-based eligibility, it sets forth new restrictions and requirements for such programs. For example, the act prohibits a Reserve Bank from lending to an insolvent firm through a broad-based program or creating a program designed to remove assets from a single and specific institution's balance sheet.[102] According to Federal Reserve Board staff, under its current Section 13(3) authority, the Federal Reserve Board could re-launch emergency programs to assist the repurchase agreement, commercial paper, and other credit markets, if these markets became severely strained and if the program is broad-based and meets the other requirements imposed by the Dodd-Frank Act. The Dodd-Frank Act also includes additional

---

[101]§ 1101(a), 124 Stat. at 2113.

[102]§ 1101(a)(6), 124 Stat. at 2114 (codified at 12 U.S.C. § 343(B)(ii)-(iii)).

transparency and reporting requirements should the Federal Reserve Board exercise its Section 13(3) authority.[103]

Although the Dodd-Frank Act requires the Federal Reserve Board to promulgate regulations that establish policies and procedures governing any future lending under Section 13(3) authority, Federal Reserve Board officials told us that they have not yet completed the process for drafting these policies and procedures.[104] Federal Reserve Board staff have made progress in drafting these policies and procedures by regulation, but have not set time frames for completing and publicly proposing a draft regulation. While there is no mandated deadline for completion of the procedures, the Dodd-Frank Act does require the Federal Reserve Board to establish the policies and procedures "as soon as is practicable."[105] According to a Federal Reserve Board official, in implementing its regulatory responsibilities under the Dodd-Frank Act, the Federal Reserve Board has focused first on the required regulations that have statutory deadlines and the regulations which are specifically directed at enhancing the safety and soundness of the financial system. Although the act did not set a specific deadline, the Federal Reserve Board can better ensure accountability for implementing rulemaking and more timely completion of these procedures by setting internal timelines for completing the rulemaking process. Furthermore, finalizing these policies and procedures could help the Federal Reserve Board to ensure that any future emergency lending does not assist an insolvent firm and complies with other Dodd-Frank Act requirements.

Completing these policies and procedures could also address prior recommendations we made with respect to the Federal Reserve System's emergency assistance programs.[106] For example, in our July 2011 report, we recommended that the Chairman of the Federal Reserve Board direct Federal Reserve Board and Reserve Bank staff to set forth the Federal

---

[103]§§ 1101-1103, 124 Stat. at 2113-20. These requirements include a requirement for the Federal Reserve Board to report to Congress on any loan or financial assistance authorized under Section 13(3), including the justification for the exercise of authority; the identity of the recipient; the date, amount, and form of the assistance; and the material terms of the assistance. § 1101(a)(6) (codified at 12 U.S.C. § 343(C)(i)).

[104]§ 1101(a)(6)(B)(i), 124 Stat. at 2113-14. (codified at 12 U.S.C. § 343(B)).

[105]§ 1101(a)(6)(B)(i), 124 Stat. at 2113. (codified at 12 U.S.C. § 343(B)(i)).

[106]GAO-11-696.

GAO-14-18 Government Support for Bank Holding Companies

Reserve Board's process for documenting its justification for each use of section 13(3) authority. We noted that more complete documentation could help the Federal Reserve Board ensure that it is complying with the Dodd-Frank Act's requirement on its use of this authority.[107] The Federal Reserve Board agreed that this prior report's recommendations would benefit its response to future crises and agreed to strongly consider how best to respond.

Enhanced Prudential Standards for Large Financial Firms Have Not Been Fully Implemented

The Dodd-Frank Act also introduced a number of regulatory changes designed to reduce the risks that the largest financial institutions pose to the financial system. A notable change is a set of new prudential requirements and capital standards designed to strengthen the regulatory oversight and capital base of large financial institutions.[108] The Federal Reserve Board has made progress towards implementing these enhanced regulatory standards.

The Dodd-Frank Act requires the Federal Reserve Board to create enhanced capital and prudential standards for bank holding companies with $50 billion or more in consolidated assets and nonbank financial holding companies designated by FSOC.[109] The act's provisions related to enhanced prudential standards for these covered firms include the following:

- **Risk-based capital requirements and leverage limits**. The Federal Reserve Board must establish capital and leverage standards, which as proposed would include a requirement for covered firms to develop capital plans to help ensure that they maintain capital ratios above specified standards, under both normal and adverse conditions.[110] In addition, the Federal Reserve Board has announced its intention to apply capital surcharges to some or all firms based on the risks firms pose to the financial system.

---

[107]See GAO-11-696.

[108]§§ 165-166, 124 Stat. at 1423-32.

[109]§165(a)(1), 124 Stat. at 1423.

[110]§165(b)(1)(A)(i), 124 Stat. at 1424; *Enhanced Prudential Standards and Early Remediation Requirements for Covered Companies; Proposed Rule*, 77 Fed. Reg. 594 (Jan. 5, 2012).

- **Liquidity requirements**. The Federal Reserve Board must establish liquidity standards, which as proposed would include requirements for covered firms to hold liquid assets that can be used to cover their cash outflows over short periods.[111]

- **Single-counterparty credit limits**. The Federal Reserve Board must issue rules that, in general, limit the total net credit exposure of a covered firm to any single unaffiliated company to 25 percent of its total capital stock and surplus.[112]

- **Risk management requirements**. Publicly traded covered firms must establish a risk committee and be subject to enhanced risk management standards.[113]

- **Stress testing requirements**. The Federal Reserve Board is required to conduct an annual evaluation of whether covered firms have sufficient capital to absorb losses that could arise from adverse economic conditions.[114]

- **Debt-to-equity limits**. Certain covered firms may be required to maintain a debt-to-equity ratio of no more than 15-to-1.[115]

- **Early remediation**. The Federal Reserve Board is required to establish a regulatory framework for the early remediation of financial weaknesses of covered firms in order to minimize the probability that such companies will become insolvent and the potential harm of such insolvencies to the financial stability of the United States.[116]

---

[111]§165(b)(1)(A)(ii), 124 Stat. at 1424: *Enhanced Prudential Standards and Early Remediation Requirements for Covered Companies; Proposed Rule*, 77 Fed. Reg. 594 (Jan. 5, 2012).

[112]§165(e)(2), 124 Stat. at 1427.

[113]§165(h), 124 Stat. at 1429.

[114]§165(i)(1), 124 Stat. at 1430. Companies subject to enhanced prudential standards also must conduct annual or semiannual stress tests of their own, depending on their size. § 165(i)(2), 124 Stat. at 1430-31.

[115]§165(j), 124 Stat. at 1431.

[116]§166, 124 Stat. at 1432.

Some of these rules have been finalized, while others have not. For example, in October 2012, the Federal Reserve Board issued a final rule implementing the supervisory and company-run stress test requirements.[117] In December 2012, the Federal Reserve Board issued proposed regulations designed to implement enhanced prudential standards and early remediation requirements for foreign banking organizations and foreign nonbank financial companies.[118]

The Federal Reserve Board intends to satisfy some aspects of the Dodd-Frank Act's heightened prudential standards rules for bank holding companies with total consolidated assets of $50 billion or more through implementation of the new Basel Committee on Banking Supervision standards, known as Basel III. The new standards seek to improve the quality of regulatory capital and introduce a new minimum common equity requirement. Basel III also raises the quantity and quality of capital required and introduces capital conservation and countercyclical buffers designed to better ensure that banks have sufficient capital to absorb losses in a future crisis. In addition, Basel III establishes for the first time an international leverage standard for internationally active banks.

Consistent with that intention, in July 2013 FDIC, the Federal Reserve Board, and OCC finalized a rule that revised risk-based and leverage capital requirements for banking organizations.[119] The interim final rule implements a revised definition of regulatory capital, a new common equity Tier 1 minimum capital requirement, a higher minimum Tier 1

---

[117] *Supervisory and Company-Run Stress Test Requirements for Covered Companies*, 77 Fed. Reg. 62378 (Oct. 12, 2012); 12 C.F.R. §§ 252.131-136, 252.141-138.

[118] *Enhanced Prudential Standards and Early Remediation Requirements for Foreign Banking Organizations and Foreign Nonbank Financial Companies*, 77 Fed. Reg. 76628 (Dec. 28, 2012). Additionally, rules regarding single-counterparty credit limits and risk management have been proposed but not finalized. *Enhanced Prudential Standards and Early Remediation Requirements for Covered Companies*; Proposed Rule, 77 Fed. Reg. 594 (Jan. 5, 2012).

[119] *Regulatory Capital Rules: Regulatory Capital, Implementation of Basel III, Capital Adequacy, Transition Provisions, Prompt Corrective Action, Standardized Approach for Risk-Weighted Assets, Market Discipline and Disclosure Requirements, Advanced Approaches Risk-Based Capital Rule, and Market Risk Capital Rule*, 78 Fed. Reg. 62018 (Oct. 11, 2013); 78 Fed. Reg. 55340 (Sept. 10, 2013).

capital requirement, and a supplementary leverage ratio that incorporates a broader set of exposures in the denominator.[120]

In addition, in July 2013 FDIC, the Federal Reserve Board, and OCC proposed a rule to establish a new leverage buffer.[121] Specifically, the proposed rule requires bank holding companies with more than $700 billion in consolidated total assets or $10 trillion in assets under custody to maintain a Tier 1 capital leverage buffer of at least 2 percent above the minimum supplementary leverage ratio requirement of 3 percent, for a total of 5 percent. In addition to the leverage buffer for covered bank holding companies, the proposed rule would require insured depository institutions of covered bank holding companies to meet a 6 percent supplementary leverage ratio to be considered "well capitalized" for prompt corrective action purposes.[122] The proposed rule would take effect beginning on January 1, 2018.

Conclusions

During the 2007-2009 financial crisis, federal agencies determined that expanding support to insured banks through traditional safety nets—the discount window and deposit insurance—would not be sufficient to stem disruptions to important credit markets. The Federal Reserve System, Treasury, and FDIC introduced new programs to provide general funding

---

[120]*Id.* National banking regulators classify capital as either Tier 1—currently the highest-quality form of capital and includes common equity—or Tier 2, which is weaker in absorbing losses. Tier 1, or core, capital consists primarily of common equity. Tier 2 is supplementary capital and includes limited amounts of subordinated debt, loan loss reserves, and certain other instruments.

[121]*Regulatory Capital Rules: Regulatory Capital, Enhanced Supplementary Leverage Ratio Standards for Certain Bank Holding Companies and Their Subsidiary Insured Depository Institutions*, 78 Fed. Reg. 51101 (Aug. 20, 2013).

[122]*Id.* The Federal Deposit Insurance Corporation Improvement Act of 1991, Pub. L. No. 102-242, 105 Stat. 2236, created Sections 38 and 39 of the Federal Deposit Insurance Act to improve the ability of regulators to identify and promptly address deficiencies at depository institutions—banks and thrifts—and better safeguard and minimize losses to the deposit insurance fund. Section 38 requires regulators to classify banks into one of five capital categories and take increasingly severe actions, known as prompt corrective action, as a bank's capital deteriorates. Section 38 primarily focuses on capital as an indicator of bank health; therefore, supervisory actions under it are designed to address a bank's deteriorating capital level. Section 39 requires the banking regulators to prescribe safety and soundness standards related to noncapital criteria, including operations and management; compensation; and asset quality, earnings, and stock valuation. Section 39 allows the regulators to take action if a bank fails to meet one or more of these standards.

support to the financial sector, and some of these programs provided support at the bank holding company level or directly to nonbank financial institutions. These programs helped to improve financial conditions, and bank holding companies and their subsidiaries also experienced individual benefits from participating in particular programs, including liquidity benefits from programs that allowed them to borrow at lower interest rates and at longer maturities than might have been available in the markets. In addition, the Federal Reserve Board granted exemptions to allow banks to channel additional funding support to nonbank financial firms that lacked direct access to the federal safety nets for insured depository institutions. Government assistance to prevent the failures of large financial institutions—such as Fannie Mae, Freddie Mac, and AIG— also benefited bank holding companies, their subsidiaries, and other firms that had large risk exposures to these institutions. While these actions collectively helped to avert a more severe crisis, they raised concerns about moral hazard and the appropriate scope of federal safety nets for the financial sector.

The Dodd-Frank Act contains provisions that aim to restrict future government support for financial institutions, but the effectiveness of these provisions will depend in large part on how agencies implement them. Among other things, the act places new restrictions on the Federal Reserve Board and FDIC's emergency authorities and grants FDIC new resolution authority to resolve a large failing institution outside of the bankruptcy process. While the act continues to allow the Federal Reserve Board to use its authority under Section 13(3) of the Federal Reserve Act to authorize programs with broad-based eligibility, it sets forth new restrictions and requirements for such programs, including a requirement that lending not assist insolvent firms. The act also requires the Federal Reserve Board to establish policies and procedures governing future actions under this authority. As of the date of this report, the Federal Reserve Board has not yet completed its process for drafting these policies and procedures and has not set time frames for doing so. A Federal Reserve Board official indicated that the Board of Governors has focused first on completion of other required regulations that have statutory deadlines and the regulations that are specifically directed at enhancing the safety and soundness of the U.S. financial system. While the act did not set a specific deadline, setting time frames could help ensure more timely completion of these policies and procedures. Moreover, finalizing these procedures could help the Federal Reserve Board to ensure that any future emergency lending does not assist a failing firm and complies with other new requirements. Consistent with the changes to Federal Reserve Board authorities, the act removes FDIC's authority to provide open bank assistance under the systemic risk exception while allowing FDIC (subject to congressional approval) to provide certain assistance through a broadly available program. FDIC continues to work to implement its new resolution authority. The viability and credibility of its resolution process as an alternative to placing a systemically important firm into bankruptcy is a critical part of removing market expectations of future extraordinary government assistance. The act also contains provisions to limit the scope of financial transactions that benefit from access to federal safety nets, although it remains to be seen how these provisions will be implemented. For example, the act could result in fewer regulatory exemptions allowing banks to provide additional funding to their nonbank affiliates. Finally, certain provisions of the act that require the Federal Reserve Board to subject the largest financial firms to heightened prudential standards have not been fully implemented but could reduce the risks that those institutions pose to the financial system.

Recommendation for Executive Action

To better ensure that the design and implementation of any future emergency lending programs comply with Dodd-Frank Act requirements in a timely manner, we recommend that the Chairman of the Board of Governors of the Federal Reserve System set timeframes for completing the process for drafting policies and procedures governing the use of emergency lending authority under Section 13(3) of the Federal Reserve Act.

Agency Comments and Our Evaluation

We provided copies of this draft report to the FDIC, the Federal Reserve Board, FSOC, OCC, and Treasury for their review and comment. We also provided excerpts of the draft report for technical comment to the Federal Housing Finance Agency. All of the agencies provided technical comments, which we have incorporated, as appropriate.

In its written comments, which are reprinted in appendix V, the Federal Reserve Board accepted our recommendation and noted that it has made progress toward completing draft policies and procedures governing the use of its emergency lending authority under Section 13(3) of the Federal Reserve Act. The Federal Reserve Board's letter referred to its Chairman's July 2013 remarks on the status of these efforts. The Chairman said that he was hopeful that a final product would be completed relatively soon, perhaps by the end of this year. He further noted that in the meantime, the law is clear about what the Federal Reserve Board can and cannot do. Based on these remarks, we conducted further audit work at the Federal Reserve Board and revised our draft to include additional information about the Federal Reserve Board's progress towards drafting the required policies and procedures. While the Federal Reserve Board has made progress on a draft regulation, it has not set timeframes for completing the drafting process and issuing a final regulation. Setting timeframes for completing draft and final policies and procedures would help to ensure more timely completion of the rulemaking process. Furthermore, while certain restrictions outlined in the act may not require clarification by rulemaking, the Dodd-Frank Act explicitly directs the Federal Reserve Board to draft policies and procedures to help ensure that it complies with the full set of new restrictions and requirements the act imposes on its emergency lending authority.

In its response, the Federal Reserve Board also noted that Federal Reserve System and FDIC assistance was repaid with interest and suggested that it would be helpful for GAO, perhaps in a future report, to analyze the offsetting costs paid by financial institutions assisted through the emergency programs. We note that our draft report contained some information and analyses related to such offsetting costs. In table 1 on pages 14 through 16, we describe the key terms of selected broad-based programs, including interest, fees, and dividends that participating institutions were required to pay for this assistance. Furthermore, our draft report noted that one indicator of the extent to which an institution benefitted from participation in an emergency government program is the relative price of estimated market alternatives to the program. On pages 21 through 29, we report the results of our analyses of the pricing terms of some of the largest programs that provided funding support to bank holding companies and other eligible financial institutions. While past GAO reports have reported on the income earned by the Federal Reserve System, FDIC, and Treasury on their crisis interventions, this information is not relevant to this report's discussion of the support that bank holding companies received during the government's attempt to stabilize the financial system. As we discussed, these government interventions helped to avert a more severe crisis, but raised questions about moral hazard as market participants may expect similar emergency actions in future crises.

Treasury also provided written comments, which are reprinted in appendix VI. Treasury noted that the emergency programs discussed in the report were necessary to prevent a collapse of the financial system and that they created economic benefits not only for individual firms, large and small, but also for the financial system and the broader economy.

Treasury also observed that the Dodd-Frank Act reforms discussed in our draft report were consistent with its commitment to ending "too big to fail." In separate comments provided via email, Treasury and FSOC provided suggestions related to the report's analyses of the pricing and utilization of selected emergency programs. In response to these suggestions, we added additional information about the exclusion of observations from our pricing analyses, and added data on average assets per institution to Table 3 in appendix IV, among other changes. Treasury and FSOC also suggested that GAO consider using different benchmarks for analyzing the pricing for the Federal Reserve System's CPFF and FDIC's DGP. While analyses of these suggested benchmarks (short-dated bond prices for CPFF and 2-3 year bond prices for DGP borrowers) could provide useful insights into the robustness of our results, these analyses also have limitations and would not necessarily improve on the analyses of the benchmarks that we conducted. We concluded that the analyses included in our report are appropriate. As noted in the report, while these analyses have limitations, we determined that they are sufficient for our purposes. We note that Federal Reserve System and FDIC staff with whom we discussed our selected benchmarks for these programs agreed that the benchmarks we used in our pricing analysis are appropriate.

We are sending copies of this report to FDIC, the Federal Reserve Board, FSOC, OCC, Treasury, interested congressional committees, members, and others. In addition, the report is available at no charge on the GAO website at http://www.gao.gov.

If you or your staffs have any questions regarding this report, please contact me at (202) 512-8678 or EvansL@gao.gov. Contact points for our Offices of Congressional Relations and Public Affairs may be found on the last page of this report. GAO staff who made major contributions to this report are listed in appendix VII.

Lawrance L. Evans, Jr.
Director, Financial Markets
and Community Investment

Appendix I: Objectives, Scope and Methodology

The objectives of our report were to examine: (1) support banks and bank holding companies received as a result of government efforts to stabilize financial markets during the financial crisis of 2007-2009; and (2) recent statutory and regulatory changes related to government support for banks and bank holding companies and factors that could impact the effectiveness of these changes. In terms of scope, the first section of this report addresses benefits that bank holding companies and their subsidiaries received during the crisis from actual government support provided through emergency actions. It does not address benefits that some financial institutions may have received and may continue to receive from perceived government support. In a second report to be issued in 2014, we will report the results of our examination into whether the largest bank holding companies have received funding cost or other economic advantages as a result of expectations that the government would not allow them to fail.

To address our first objective, we reviewed documents from financial regulatory agencies—the Board of Governors of the Federal Reserve System (Federal Reserve Board), the Federal Deposit Insurance Corporation (FDIC), and the Department of the Treasury (Treasury) and analyzed agency data on emergency government actions to stabilize financial markets. Our review focused on (1) emergency government programs that provided funding support to bank holding companies or their subsidiaries as well as other eligible financial institutions, (2) government actions that provided extraordinary assistance to individual financial institutions, and (3) regulatory exemptions that allowed banks to engage in certain transactions with their nonbank affiliates. To identify the programs that provided the most significant funding support directly to bank holding companies or their subsidiaries, we reviewed program eligibility rules and data on program participation for programs created during the 2007-2009 financial crisis by Treasury, FDIC, and the Federal Reserve System.[1] Specifically, we identified a set of emergency programs created during the crisis that provided at least $10 billion in direct funding support to bank holding companies or their subsidiaries.

---

[1]The Federal Reserve System consists of the Board of Governors of the Federal Reserve System—a federal agency—and 12 regional Reserve Banks. The Federal Reserve Board has delegated some of its responsibilities for supervision and regulation to the Reserve Banks. The Federal Reserve Act authorizes the Reserve Banks to make discount window loans to the extent authorized by the Federal Reserve Board. Pub. L. No. 63-43, §§ 10B, 13, 38 Stat. 251 (codified at 12 U.S.C. §§ 347b(a), 343).

We determined that these programs included Treasury's Capital
Purchase Program (CPP); FDIC's Temporary Liquidity Guarantee
Program (TLGP); and the Federal Reserve System's Term Auction
Facility (TAF), Primary Dealer Credit Facility (PDCF), Term Securities
Lending Facility (TSLF), and Commercial Paper Funding Facility (CPFF).[2]
To describe the purpose, terms, and conditions of these programs and
other emergency government actions discussed in our first objective, we
reviewed agency documents and included information and analyses from
prior GAO work on the Troubled Asset Relief Program (TARP), the
Federal Reserve System's emergency programs, and other emergency
assistance provided to the financial sector. To obtain perspectives on the
benefits that bank holding companies received from emergency
government actions, we reviewed papers by staff of regulators and other
subject-matter experts and interviewed federal financial regulators,
representatives of bank holding companies that received emergency
government assistance, and academics. For the Federal Reserve System
and FDIC programs that were among the programs that provided the
most significant funding support, we compared the pricing and terms of
this assistance (such as interest rates and fees) to indicators of funding
market conditions during normal and crisis conditions. While this analysis
provides a measure of program pricing versus potential market
alternatives, it does not produce a precise quantification of the benefits
that accrued to participating financial institutions. To determine the extent
to which emergency equity support programs, CPP and the Targeted
Investment Program (TIP), were priced more generously than estimated
market alternatives, we reviewed estimates of the expected budget cost
associated with equity funding support programs as well as a valuation

---

[2]We reviewed prior GAO work on other emergency government programs that may have
provided benefits to bank holding companies or their subsidiaries. For example,
Treasury's Money Market Mutual Fund Guarantee Program and the Federal Reserve
System's AMLF provided support to money market mutual funds. In the absence of these
programs, money market mutual funds might have reduced their purchases of money
market instruments issued by bank holding companies, their subsidiaries, and other firms,
thereby exacerbating funding pressures on these firms. Other significant government
programs included the Term Asset-Backed Securities Loan Facility (TALF), which was
created by the Federal Reserve System and Treasury to support certain securitization
markets, and other programs created by Treasury under TARP authority. For more
information about TALF, see GAO, *Troubled Asset Relief Program: Treasury Needs to
Strengthen Its Decision-Making Process on the Term Asset-Backed Securities Loan
Facility*, GAO-10-25 (Washington, D.C.: Feb. 5, 2010). For more information about CPP
and other TARP programs, see GAO, *Troubled Asset Relief Program: One Year Later,
Actions Are Needed to Address Remaining Transparency and Accountability Challenges*,
GAO-10-16 (Washington, D.C.: Oct. 8, 2009).

analysis commissioned by the Congressional Oversight Panel (COP).
For more information about the methodology for our analysis of the
pricing and terms of these programs and associated limitations, see
appendix III. For programs that provided the most significant direct
funding support, to compare the extent to which banking organizations of
various sizes used these emergency programs, we calculated the
percentage of banking organization assets that were supported by
emergency programs—either through capital injections, loans, or
guarantees—at quarter-end dates for 2008 through 2012. For more
information about our methodology for analyzing program utilization, see
appendix IV. Finally, we obtained and analyzed Federal Reserve Board
documentation of Federal Reserve Board decisions to grant exemptions
to Section 23A of the Federal Reserve Act and approve applications from
financial companies to convert to bank holding company status.[3]

To address our second objective, we identified and reviewed relevant
statutory provisions, regulations, and agency documents. To identify
recent statutory and regulatory changes related to government support for
banks and bank holding companies, we reviewed sections of the Dodd-
Frank Wall Street Reform and Consumer Protection Act (Dodd-Frank Act)
that change rules or create new requirements for safety net programs for
insured depository institutions; further restrict the types of financial
activities that can be conducted by insured depository institutions or their
holding companies; make changes to agencies' emergency authorities to
assist or resolve financial institutions; and subject the largest bank
holding companies to enhanced regulatory oversight and standards.[4] To
corroborate our selection of Dodd-Frank Act provisions, we obtained the
views of regulatory officials and financial markets experts on the
provisions that are related to government support for banks and bank
holding companies. To update the status of agencies' efforts to implement
these provisions, we reviewed agencies' proposed and final rules, and
interviewed staff from FDIC, the Federal Reserve Board, the Office of the
Comptroller of the Currency, and Treasury. We also reviewed relevant
congressional testimonies and other public statements by agency
officials. We identified statutory provisions or requirements that agencies
had not fully implemented and interviewed agency staff about planned
steps to complete implementation. To describe factors that could impact

---

[3]Pub. L. No. 63-43, § 23A, 38 Stat. 251, 272 (1913) (12 U.S.C. § 371c).

[4]See generally Pub. L. No. 111-203, 124 Stat. 1376 (2010).

the effectiveness of relevant provisions, we reviewed prior GAO work on
the potential impacts of Dodd-Frank Act provisions. To obtain additional
perspectives on factors that could impact the effectiveness of these
provisions, we interviewed and reviewed the public statements and
analyses of agency officials, academics, and market experts.

For parts of our work that involved the analysis of computer-processed
data, we assessed the reliability of these data and determined that they
were sufficiently reliable for our purposes. Data sets for which we
conducted data reliability assessments include Federal Reserve Board
transaction data for TAF, PDCF, TSLF, and CPFF; Treasury transaction
data for CPP and TIP; and FDIC transaction data for TLGP programs (the
Debt Guarantee Program and the Transaction Account Guarantee
Program). We have relied on Federal Reserve Board and Treasury
transaction data for their respective emergency programs for past reports,
and we determined that these data were sufficiently reliable for the
purpose of presenting and analyzing the pricing and utilization of these
programs. To assess the reliability of FDIC's TLGP data, we interviewed
FDIC staff about steps they took to maintain the integrity and reliability of
program data. We also assessed the reliability of data sources used to
provide indicators of the pricing and terms for market alternatives that
could have been available to institutions that participated in these
programs. These data sources were interbank interest rates (the London
Interbank Offered Rate), additional interest rates from the Federal
Reserve, credit default swap spreads from Bloomberg, repurchase
agreement interest rates from IHS Global Insight, and repurchase
agreement haircuts from the Federal Reserve Bank of New York. To
assess the reliability of these data we took a number of steps including
inspecting data for missing observations, corroborating interest rate data
with other sources, and discussing data with agency officials. We
determined these data were sufficiently reliable for measuring market
alternatives that might have been available to participants in emergency
programs. To calculate the average percentage of assets supported by
emergency programs for banking organizations of different sizes, in
addition to the program transaction data discussed above, we used Y-9
data for bank holding companies from the Federal Reserve Bank of
Chicago, demographic data for bank holding companies and other
emergency program participants from the Federal Reserve System's
National Information Center and SNL Financial, balance sheet and
demographic data for depository institutions from FDIC, and gross
domestic product price index data from the Bureau of Economic Analysis.
To assess the reliability of these data, we reviewed relevant
documentation. In addition, for the Y-9 data for bank holding companies

from the Federal Reserve Bank of Chicago and the balance sheet data
for depository institutions from FDIC, we conducted electronic testing of
key variables.

We conducted this performance audit from January 2013 through
November 2013 in accordance with generally accepted government
auditing standards. Those standards require that we plan and perform the
audit to obtain sufficient, appropriate evidence to provide a reasonable
basis for our findings and conclusions based on our audit objectives. We
believe that the evidence obtained provides a reasonable basis for our
findings and conclusions based on our audit objectives.

Appendix II: Overview of Selected Federal Government Programs That Provided Emergency Funding Support to Banking Entities during the 2007-2009 Financial Crisis

During the financial crisis, the Federal Reserve System, Treasury, and FDIC introduced new programs with broad-based eligibility to provide general funding support to the banking sector and stabilize the financial system. Federal government interventions that provided the most significant direct funding support to U.S. bank holding companies or their subsidiaries were:

- the Federal Reserve System's credit and liquidity programs;[1]
- Treasury's capital investments through the Troubled Asset Relief Program; and
- FDIC's guarantees of certain newly issued debt and previously uninsured deposits through the Temporary Liquidity Guarantee Program (TLGP).

The first of these interventions occurred in late 2007 when the Federal Reserve System modified discount window terms and launched a new program to auction discount window loans to banks to address strains in interbank credit markets.

- *Discount window.* In August 2007, the cost of term funding (loans provided at terms of 1 month or longer) spiked suddenly—primarily due to investor concerns about banks' actual exposures to various mortgage-related securities—and commercial banks increasingly had to borrow overnight to meet their funding needs.[2] The Federal Reserve Board feared that the disorderly functioning of interbank lending markets would impair the ability of commercial banks to provide credit to households and businesses. To ease stresses in these markets, on August 17, 2007, the Federal Reserve Board approved two temporary changes to discount window terms: (1) a reduction of the discount rate—the interest rate at which the Reserve

---

[1]This report focuses on the Federal Reserve System's programs that provided the most significant direct funding support to bank holding companies and their subsidiaries. For a broader discussion of the Federal Reserve System's emergency actions during the crisis, see GAO, *Federal Reserve System: Opportunities Exist to Strengthen Policies and Processes for Managing Emergency Assistance,* GAO-11-696 (Washington, D.C.: July 21, 2011).

[2]The sudden spike in the cost of term funding followed the August 9, 2007, announcement by BNP Paribas, a large banking organization based in France, that it could not value certain mortgage-related assets in three of its investment funds because of a lack of liquidity in U.S. securitization markets. Greater reliance on overnight borrowing increased the volatility of banks' funding costs and increased "rollover" risk, or the risk that banks would not be able to renew their funding as loans matured.

Banks extended collateralized loans at the discount window—by 50 basis points; and (2) an extension of the discount window lending term from overnight to up to 30 days, with the possibility of renewal.[3] This change initially resulted in little additional borrowing from the discount window. After subsiding in October 2007, tensions in term funding markets reappeared in late November, possibly driven by a seasonal contraction in the supply of year-end funding.

- *Term Auction Facility (TAF)*. On December 12, 2007, the Federal Reserve Board announced the creation of TAF to address continuing disruptions in U.S. term interbank lending markets.[4] TAF provided term funding to depository institutions eligible to borrow from the discount window.[5] In contrast to the traditional discount window program, which loaned funds to individual institutions at the discount rate, TAF auctioned loans to many eligible institutions at once at a market-determined interest rate. Federal Reserve Board officials noted that one important advantage of this auction approach was that it could address concerns among eligible borrowers about the perceived stigma of discount window borrowing. TAF was the largest Federal Reserve System emergency program in terms of the dollar amount of funding support provided, with TAF loans outstanding peaking at $493 billion in March 2009.

In March 2008, the Federal Reserve Board invoked its emergency authority under Section 13(3) of the Federal Reserve Act to authorize two new programs to support repurchase agreement markets—large, short-term collateralized funding markets—that many financial institutions rely

---

[3]One basis point is equivalent to 0.01 percent or 1/100th of a percent. The Federal Reserve Board later approved further reductions in the discount rate and increased the maximum maturity of discount window loans to 90 days. In addition to the discount window changes, starting in September 2007, the Federal Open Market Committee (FOMC) announced a series of reductions in the target federal funds rate—the FOMC-established target interest rate that banks charge each other for loans.

[4]The Federal Reserve Board authorized Reserve Banks to extend credit through TAF by revising the regulations governing Reserve Bank discount window lending.

[5]Section 10B of the Federal Reserve Act provides the Reserve Banks broad authority to extend credit to depository institutions. 12 U.S.C. § 347b.

on to finance a wide range of securities.[6] The Federal Reserve Board
limited eligibility for these programs to the primary dealers, a designated
group of broker-dealers and banks that transact with the Federal Reserve
Bank of New York (FRBNY) in its conduct of open market operations.[7]
Many of the primary dealers are subsidiaries of U.S. bank holding
companies or large foreign banking organizations.

- *Term Securities Lending Facility (TSLF)*. On March 11, 2008, the
  Federal Reserve Board announced the creation of TSLF to auction
  28-day loans of U.S. Treasury securities to primary dealers to
  increase the amount of high-quality collateral available for these
  dealers to borrow against in the repurchase agreement markets. In
  early March, the Federal Reserve Board found that repurchase
  agreement lenders were requiring higher haircuts for loans against a
  range of securities and were becoming reluctant to lend against
  mortgage-related securities. As a result, many financial institutions
  increasingly had to rely on higher-quality collateral, such as U.S.
  Treasury securities, to obtain cash in these markets, and a shortage
  of such high quality collateral emerged. Through competitive auctions
  that allowed dealers to bid a fee to exchange harder-to-finance
  collateral for easier-to-finance Treasury securities, TSLF was intended
  to promote confidence among lenders and to reduce the need for
  dealers to sell illiquid assets into the markets, which could have
  further depressed the prices of these assets. The market value of

---

[6]Under a repurchase agreement, a borrowing institution generally acquires funds by
selling securities to a lending institution and agreeing to repurchase the securities after a
specified time at a given price. The securities, in effect, are collateral provided by the
borrower to the lender. In the event of a borrower's default on the repurchase transaction,
the lender would be able to take (and sell) the collateral provided by the borrower.
Lenders typically will not provide a loan for the full market value of the posted securities,
and the difference between the values of the securities and the loan is called a margin or
haircut. This deduction is intended to protect the lenders against a decline in the price of
the securities provided as collateral. When the market value of assets used to secure or
collateralize repurchase transactions declines, borrowers are usually required to post
additional collateral.

[7]The Federal Reserve System conducts open market operations to influence the amount
of money and credit available in the economy. FRBNY carries out directives from the
Federal Open Market Committee—which consists of members of the Board of Governors
and the FRBNY president, and four other Reserve Bank presidents who serve on a
rotating basis—by engaging in purchase or sales of certain securities, typically U.S.
government securities, in the secondary market. FRBNY conducts these transactions
through the primary dealers.

GAO-14-18 Government Support for Bank Holding Companies

TSLF securities loans outstanding peaked at $236 billion in October 2008.

- *Primary Dealer Credit Facility (PDCF).* On March 16, 2008, the Federal Reserve Board announced the creation of PDCF to provide overnight collateralized cash loans to the primary dealers. In the days following the March 11 announcement of TSLF, one of the primary dealers, Bear Stearns, experienced a run on its liquidity.[8] Because the first TSLF auction would not be held until later that month, Federal Reserve Board and FRBNY staff worked to ready PDCF for launch by Monday, March 17, 2008, when Federal Reserve Board officials feared a Bear Stearns bankruptcy announcement might trigger runs on the liquidity of other primary dealers. Although the Bear Stearns bankruptcy was averted, PDCF commenced operation on March 17, 2008.[9] Eligible PDCF collateral initially included collateral eligible for open-market operations as well as investment-grade corporate securities, municipal securities, and asset-backed securities, including private label mortgage-backed securities. The Federal Reserve Board later expanded eligible collateral types for both TSLF and PDCF.

In late 2008, the bankruptcy of Lehman Brothers triggered an intensification of the crisis and the Federal Reserve System, Treasury and FDIC took a range of new actions to provide additional support to financial institutions and key credit markets.

- Federal Reserve System actions. In September and October 2008, the Federal Reserve Board modified its existing programs, launched new programs, and took other actions to address worsening market conditions.

    - *Modifications to TSLF, PDCF, and TAF.* On September 14, 2008, shortly before Lehman Brothers announced it would file for bankruptcy, the Federal Reserve Board announced changes to TSLF and PDCF to provide expanded liquidity support to primary

---

[8]Federal Reserve Board officials noted that although TSLF was announced to address market tensions impacting many firms, some market participants concluded that its establishment was driven by specific concerns about Bear Stearns.

[9]As discussed later in this section, the Federal Reserve Board used its emergency authority to authorize an emergency overnight loan and other assistance to avoid a disorderly failure of Bear Stearns.

dealers. Specifically, the Federal Reserve Board announced that TSLF-eligible collateral would be expanded to include all investment-grade debt securities and PDCF-eligible collateral would be expanded to include all securities eligible to be pledged in the tri-party repurchase agreements system, including noninvestment grade securities and equities.[10] On September 29, 2008, the Federal Reserve Board also announced expanded support through TAF by doubling the amount of funds that would be available in each TAF auction cycle from $150 billion to $300 billion.

- *Commercial Paper Funding Facility (CPFF)*. On October 7, 2008, the Federal Reserve Board announced the creation of CPFF under its Section 13(3) authority to provide a liquidity backstop to U.S. issuers of commercial paper. Commercial paper is an important source of short-term funding for U.S. financial and nonfinancial businesses.[11] CPFF became operational on October 27, 2008, and was operated by FRBNY. In the weeks leading up to CPFF's announcement, the commercial paper markets showed signs of strain: the volume of commercial paper outstanding declined, interest rates on longer-term commercial paper increased significantly, and increasing amounts of commercial paper were issued on an overnight basis as money-market funds and other investors became reluctant to purchase commercial paper at longer-dated maturities. By standing ready to purchase eligible commercial paper, CPFF was intended to eliminate much of the risk that commercial paper issuers would be unable to issue new commercial paper to replace their maturing commercial paper obligations.

---

[10]For TSLF, previously, only Treasury securities, agency securities, and AAA-rated mortgage-backed and asset-backed securities could be pledged. For PDCF, previously, eligible collateral had to have at least an investment-grade rating. Tri-party repurchase agreements include three parties: the borrower, the lender, and a tri-party agent that facilitates the repurchase agreement transaction by providing custody of the securities posted as collateral and valuing the collateral, among other services.

[11]There are two main types of commercial paper: unsecured and asset-backed. Unsecured paper is not backed by collateral and the credit rating of the issuing institution is a key variable in determining the cost of its issuance. In contrast, Asset Backed Commercial Paper is collateralized by assets and therefore is a secured form of borrowing.

- *Other actions.* The Federal Reserve System launched other new programs that provided liquidity support for other market participants, but did not serve a major source of direct support for U.S. bank holding companies or their subsidiaries.[12]

- *Troubled Asset Relief Program.* On October 3, 2008, the Emergency Economic Stabilization Act of 2008 (EESA) was signed into law to help stem the financial crisis.[13] EESA provided Treasury with the authority to create the Troubled Asset Relief Program (TARP), under which it could buy or guarantee up to almost $700 billion of the "troubled assets" that it deemed to be at the heart of the crisis, including mortgages, mortgage-backed securities, and any other financial instruments, such as equity investments. Treasury created the Capital Purchase Program (CPP) in October 2008 to provide capital to viable financial institutions by using its authority to purchase preferred shares and subordinated debt. In return for its investments, Treasury received dividend or interest payments and warrants.[14] On October 14, 2008, Treasury allocated $250 billion of the original $700 billion in overall TARP funds for CPP. The allocation was subsequently reduced in March 2009 to reflect lower estimated funding needs, as evidenced by actual participation rates. The program was closed to new investments on December 31, 2009. Smaller capital infusion programs included the Targeted Investment Program (TIP) and the Community Development Capital Initiative (CDCI).

- *Temporary Liquidity Guarantee Program.* In October 2008, FDIC created TLGP to complement the Federal Reserve and Treasury programs in restoring confidence in financial institutions and repairing their capacity to meet the credit needs of American households and

---

[12]These programs included the AMLF and the Term Asset-Backed Securities Loan Facility. For more information about these programs, see GAO-11-696.

[13]Pub. L. No. 110-343, Div. A, 122 Stat. 3765 (codified at 12 U.S.C. §§ 5201-5261). EESA established the Office of Financial Stability within Treasury and provided it with broad, flexible authorities to buy or guarantee troubled mortgage-related assets or any other financial instruments necessary to stabilize the financial markets. *Id.* at § 101 (12 U.S.C. § 5211).

[14]A warrant is an option to buy shares of common stock or preferred stock at a predetermined price on or before a specified date.

businesses.[15] TLGP's Debt Guarantee Program (DGP) was designed to improve liquidity in term-funding markets by guaranteeing certain newly issued senior unsecured debt of financial institutions and their holding companies. By guaranteeing payment of these debt obligations, DGP was intended to address the difficulty that creditworthy institutions were facing in replacing maturing debt because of risk aversion in the markets. TLGP's Transaction Account Guarantee Program (TAGP) also was created to stabilize an important source of liquidity for many financial institutions. TAGP temporarily extended an unlimited deposit guarantee to certain noninterest-bearing transaction accounts to assure holders of the safety of these deposits and limit further outflows. By facilitating access to borrowed funds at lower rates, Treasury, FDIC, and the Federal Reserve expected TLGP to free up funding for banks to make loans to creditworthy businesses and consumers. Furthermore, by promoting stable funding sources for financial institutions, they intended TLGP to help avert bank and thrift failures that would impose costs on the insurance fund and taxpayers and potentially contribute to a worsening of the crisis.

---

[15]TLGP's authorization required a systemic risk determination by the Secretary of the Treasury. For more information about this determination, see GAO, *Federal Deposit Insurance Act: Regulators' Use of Systemic Risk Exception Raises Moral Hazard Concerns and Opportunities Exist to Clarify the Provision*, GAO-10-100 (Washington, D.C.: April 15, 2010).

Appendix III: Methodology for Analysis of Pricing and Terms for Financial Stability Programs

Although imperfect, one indicator of the extent to which an institution benefited from participation in an emergency program is the relative price of estimated market alternatives to the program. To determine how pricing of the emergency assistance compared to market rates, we compared the interest rates and fees charged by the Federal Reserve and FDIC for participation in the emergency lending and guarantee programs with market alternatives that might have been available to program participants. We considered a number of potential indicators of market interest rates available to financial institutions, including a survey of interbank interest rates (the London Interbank Offered Rate or LIBOR), commercial paper interest rates published by the Federal Reserve Board, spreads on bank credit default swaps (CDS), and interest rates on repurchase agreements. These interest rates and spreads provide a general indication of market alternatives available to participants but are imperfect and hence unlikely to reflect available alternatives for all participants at all points in time. For example, participants' access to market alternatives may have been limited, there may be only limited data on the relevant private market, or market alternatives could vary across participants in ways that we do not observe in the data. Furthermore, once programs were introduced, they probably influenced the price of market alternatives, making it difficult to interpret differences between program pricing to contemporary market pricing while programs were active. Where possible—when programs had pricing rules (PDCF, CPFF, and DGP)—we applied program pricing rules during time periods that were not influenced by the program itself to compare program pricing with counterfactual market prices. By choosing high and low financial stress time periods, we can estimate the extent to which participants may have benefitted from program pricing during the financial crisis as well as the extent to which program pricing became less attractive as financial conditions returned to normal.

Programs with auction-based pricing (TAF and TSLF) raise particular challenges in interpreting differences between program pricing and market pricing. Under certain assumptions, bidders would bid program pricing up to their market alternatives, which could limit potential benefits from the program as well as eliminate any difference between program and market pricing.[1] In addition, without a pricing rule we cannot apply

---

[1] However, the quantity of funds made available in the auction could also reduce prices in the alternative market, which would provide benefits to participants and nonparticipants alike. The size of the benefit in this instance would also be difficult to measure.

GAO-14-18 Government Support for Bank Holding Companies

Appendix III: Methodology for Analysis of
Pricing and Terms for Financial Stability
Programs

pricing for auction-based programs to high or low financial stress time periods not influenced by the program itself—in other words, contemporaneous pricing is contaminated by the program itself, making it difficult to determine the true market alternative. As a result, deviations between program and market pricing could indicate differences in terms rather than a benefit to participating financial institutions. These challenges suggest that our estimates of the difference between program and market pricing for auction-based programs should be interpreted with caution. TAF and TSLF also had minimum pricing determined by the Federal Reserve that was prescribed when auctions were undersubscribed. In these instances prices were no longer auction-determined in the traditional sense although the outcome of the auction (undersubscription) determined when the minimum pricing would apply.

It is important to note that, among other limitations, our indicators do not capture all the benefits associated with program participation. Because our proxies for market alternatives are imperfect, market prices appear on occasion to be lower than emergency program pricing despite significant participation by financial institutions at these times. Participation by itself suggests that program prices and/or terms were relatively attractive in comparison to available alternatives—benefits could arise from price, quantity available, or other nonprice characteristics of the assistance (loan term, eligible collateral, etc.). Therefore, we discarded values of spreads between program pricing and market alternatives when they were zero or negative since negative spreads are unlikely to capture the benefits that accrued to participants. If these truly reflected market alternatives for the pool of potential participants, then there would be no participation or the participation would have been based on other nonprice considerations. We assume that the true (unobserved) market alternatives overlap at times with our observed proxies. At other times the market alternatives we are able to observe and measure may not overlap with the true market alternatives for participants (including when observed market alternatives indicate programs are more expensive than market rates).

Because PDCF operated similarly to repurchase agreement markets, we compared collateral haircuts in PDCF with select asset classes in the triparty (intermediated by a clearing bank) repurchase agreement markets. We selected those asset classes where we were able to draw clear parallels between categories of collateral allowed under PDCF and categories identified in data based on private repurchase agreement market we received from the Federal Reserve Bank of New York. The haircut is an important loan term in repurchase agreement contracts and

Appendix III: Methodology for Analysis of
Pricing and Terms for Financial Stability
Programs

collateralized lending, the amount of additional collateral required over the value of the loan that is required to secure the loan. Securities with greater risk or less liquidity generally have larger haircuts (i.e., more collateral is required). PDCF borrowers might have utilized triparty repurchase agreement markets for alternative sources of secured borrowing during the 2007-2009 financial crisis.

To determine the extent to which emergency equity support programs, CPP and TIP, were priced more generously than estimated market alternatives, we reviewed estimates of the expected budget cost associated with equity funding support programs as well as a valuation analysis commissioned by the Congressional Oversight Panel (COP). The benefits that accrued to banks from participation in equity funding support programs are likely to be proportional to the subsidy rates estimated for accounting purposes. Estimates of subsidy rates are based on a net present value analysis—the price and terms which are offered by a federal agency are compared to the lifetime expected cost (net present value) of the equity and the difference is known as a subsidy. Because private market participants might have charged a price based on a comparable net present value analysis, banks would have benefitted to the extent that the prices offered by Treasury for their equity exceed what they were likely to receive based on the net present value. The valuation analysis commissioned by COP explicitly compared the prices received by Treasury with market-based valuations of similar securities. We assume that the net present values estimated for accounting purposes by Treasury and CBO are reasonable proxies for the market valuations that are more directly estimated in the COP analysis. We used the earliest available estimates from the Congressional Budget Office (CBO) and Treasury as they were closest to market conditions at the time that programs were initiated. Estimates of these subsidy rates depended on timing and market conditions and the size of these subsidy rates likely fell over time as market conditions improved.

Appendix IV: Use of Financial Stability Programs by Banking Organizations of Different Sizes

Data

Emergency government programs to stabilize financial markets resulted in funding support to bank holding companies and insured depository institutions (collectively, banking organizations) of various sizes.[1] To compare use of emergency funding programs by banking organizations of different sizes, we analyzed quarterly data on bank holding companies and depository institutions for the period from 2008 to 2012 along with data on emergency program transactions that occurred during that period. We used quarterly balance sheet and demographic data on bank holding companies for the period from the first quarter of 2008 through the fourth quarter of 2012 from the Federal Reserve Bank of Chicago and the Federal Reserve System's National Information Center (NIC), quarterly balance sheet and demographic data on depository institutions from FDIC for the period from the first quarter of 2008 through the fourth quarter of 2012, and quarterly data on the GDP price index from the Bureau of Economic Analysis (BEA) for the period from the first quarter of 2008 through the fourth quarter of 2012. We also used data on Debt Guarantee Program (DGP) and TAGP transactions from FDIC, data on Commercial Paper Funding Facility, Primary Dealer Credit Facility, TAF, and TSLF transactions from the Board of Governors of the Federal Reserve System, and data on CPP and TIP transactions from the U.S. Department of the Treasury. Finally, we used demographic data on emergency funding program participants obtained from NIC and from SNL Financial.

Methodology

We organized depository institutions and bank holding companies into groups—hereafter banking organizations—based on their regulatory high holder (the highest holding company in a tiered organization), where depository institutions or bank holding companies that did not indicate a high holder are assumed to be their own high holder. We calculated consolidated assets for each banking organization, excluding banking organizations for which we cannot reliably calculate consolidated assets. We excluded banking organizations with a high holder that was not in our data, e.g., banking organizations with foreign high holders. For banking organizations with a high holder that was in our data and that included at least one bank holding company, we excluded those for which the high holder did not report consolidated assets, those for which the high holder

---

[1]Our analysis focuses on the use of emergency programs by banking organizations. However, emergency programs also provided funding for some nonbank financial institutions, such as standalone broker-dealers, and for some nonfinancial companies, such as McDonald's Corp. and Harley-Davidson.

reported consolidated assets but they were less than its parent-only assets, those for which the high holder's consolidated assets were less than consolidated assets reported by some other bank holding company in the organization, those for which none of the bank holding companies reported consolidated assets, and those that did not contain any depository institutions. For all remaining banking organizations that contained at least one bank holding company, we set consolidated assets for the group equal to consolidated assets reported by the high holder. Note that consolidated assets for a bank holding company include the assets of all consolidated subsidiaries, which generally include all companies for which the bank holding company owns more than 50 percent of the outstanding voting stock. For banking organizations with a high holder in our data that did not include a bank holding company, such as standalone depository institutions, we set consolidated assets for the banking organization equal to the depository institution's consolidated assets.

Banking organizations for which we could reliably calculate consolidated assets constitute our analysis sample. Small bank holding companies (those with assets less than $500 million) generally report their consolidated assets in the second and fourth quarters of each year, but they generally do not do so in the first and third quarters of each year. To maintain consistency in the composition of the analysis sample over time, we ultimately used results for only the second and fourth quarters of each year from 2008 to 2012. Companies that converted to bank holding companies during the crisis are included in our analysis only for the quarters for which they filed financial statements for bank holding companies with the Federal Reserve. For example, both Goldman Sachs Group, Inc. and Morgan Stanley became bank holding companies in September 2008 but neither filed form FR Y-9C, the source of our data on consolidated assets for large bank holding companies, until the first quarter of 2009. As a result, these two companies are not part of our analysis sample until 2009. We assigned banking organizations in our analysis sample to one of six size groups based on their consolidated assets, adjusted for inflation and expressed in fourth quarter 2012 dollars: less than $500 million; at least $500 million and less than $1 billion; at least $1 billion and less than $10 billion; at least $10 billion and less than $50 billion; at least $50 billion and less than $250 billion; and $250 billion or more. Table 3 shows the numbers of banking organizations in our analysis sample by size group and the numbers of banking organizations excluded from our analysis sample for the second and fourth quarters of each year from 2008 to 2012.

Table 3. Numbers and average assets of banking organizations in analysis sample by size and quarter, June 30, 2008 to December 31, 2012.

Quarter		Banking organization in analysis sample						Banking organizations excluded from analysis sample
		Assets less than $500 million	Assets $500 million to 1 billion	Assets $1 to 10 billion	Assets $10 to 50 billion	Assets $50 to 250 billion	Assets $250 billion or more	
2008q2	Number	5,824	686	536	59	20	8	256
	Average assets	$0.15	$0.69	$2.59	$19.91	$114.48	$1,089.51	—
2008q4	Number	5,746	674	546	61	15	8	269
	Average assets	$0.15	$0.69	$2.52	$19.29	$111.59	$1,134.68	—
2009q2	Number	5,687	676	554	60	18	9	264
	Average assets	$0.16	$0.69	$2.48	$18.12	$119.98	$1,184.69	—
2009q4	Number	5,595	681	540	57	19	9	264
	Average assets	$0.16	$0.69	$2.48	$18.05	$117.11	$1,183.91	—
2010q2	Number	5,520	671	528	53	20	9	261
	Average assets	$0.16	$0.69	$2.49	$18.25	$114.96	$1,207.20	—
2010q4	Number	5,448	648	520	53	20	10	262
	Average assets	$0.16	$0.69	$2.51	$18.42	$104.81	$1,123.85	—
2011q2	Number	5,377	644	512	54	19	10	255
	Average assets	$0.16	$0.69	$2.47	$19.31	$109.30	$1,144.96	—
2011q4	Number	5,287	628	514	54	18	10	256
	Average assets	$0.16	$0.69	$2.50	$19.81	$117.06	$1,119.79	—
2012q2	Number	5,215	632	506	55	17	11	251
	Average assets	$0.16	$0.69	$2.50	$19.86	$108.07	$1,055.56	—
2012q4	Number	5,076	634	505	55	16	10	248
	Average assets	$0.17	$0.69	$2.59	$20.92	$113.98	$1,091.00	—

Source: GAO analysis of BEA, FDIC, and Federal Reserve data.

Note: Assets are adjusted for inflation and expressed in fourth quarter 2012 dollars. We do not report average assets for banking organizations we excluded from the analysis sample because the banking organizations we excluded from the analysis sample are the ones for which we could not reliably calculate consolidated assets

For each banking organization in our analysis sample, we calculated the percentage of assets funded by capital provided, loans provided, and liabilities guaranteed by emergency programs at quarter-end for the second and fourth quarters of 2008 through 2012. Capital provided by emergency programs includes capital investments by Treasury under CPP and TIP. Loans provided by emergency programs include TAF, TSLF, PDCF, and CPFF loans from the Federal Reserve System. Funding guaranteed by emergency programs includes deposits guaranteed by FDIC through TAGP and debt guaranteed by FDIC through DGP. To compare the extent to which banking organizations of various sizes used emergency programs, we calculated the percentage of banking organization assets that were supported by emergency programs—either through capital injections, loans, or guarantees—at quarter-end dates from mid-2008 through the end of 2012. In addition, for each of the three types of support, we decomposed average support as a percentage of assets for banking organizations of different sizes into its two components: (1) the rate of participation in emergency programs by banking organizations of different sizes as measured by the percentage of banking organizations using funds provided or guaranteed by the emergency programs and (2) average support as a percentage of assets for those participants.

Results

Federal Reserve System programs. TAF was established in December 2007, PDCF and TSLF were established in March 2008, and CPFF began purchasing commercial paper in October 2008. As of the end of 2008, combined CPFF, PDCF, TAF, and TSLF loans outstanding ranged from about 0.01 percent of assets on average for all banking organizations with less than $500 million in assets to about 2.5 percent of assets on average for all banking organizations with at least $50 billion but less than $250 billion in assets (see fig. 3). For banking organizations with $250 billion or more in assets, combined CPFF, PDCF, TAF, and TSLF loans outstanding were about 2.0 percent of assets on average. As of mid-2009, loans outstanding for these four programs combined had declined to less than 1 percent of assets on average for banking organizations of all sizes, and as of the end of 2009, they had declined to less than half a percent of assets on average.

Figure 3: Average CPFF, PDCF, TAF, and TSLF Loan Amounts Outstanding as a Percentage of Assets at Quarter-End for Banking Organizations by Size, June 30, 2008, through December 31, 2012.

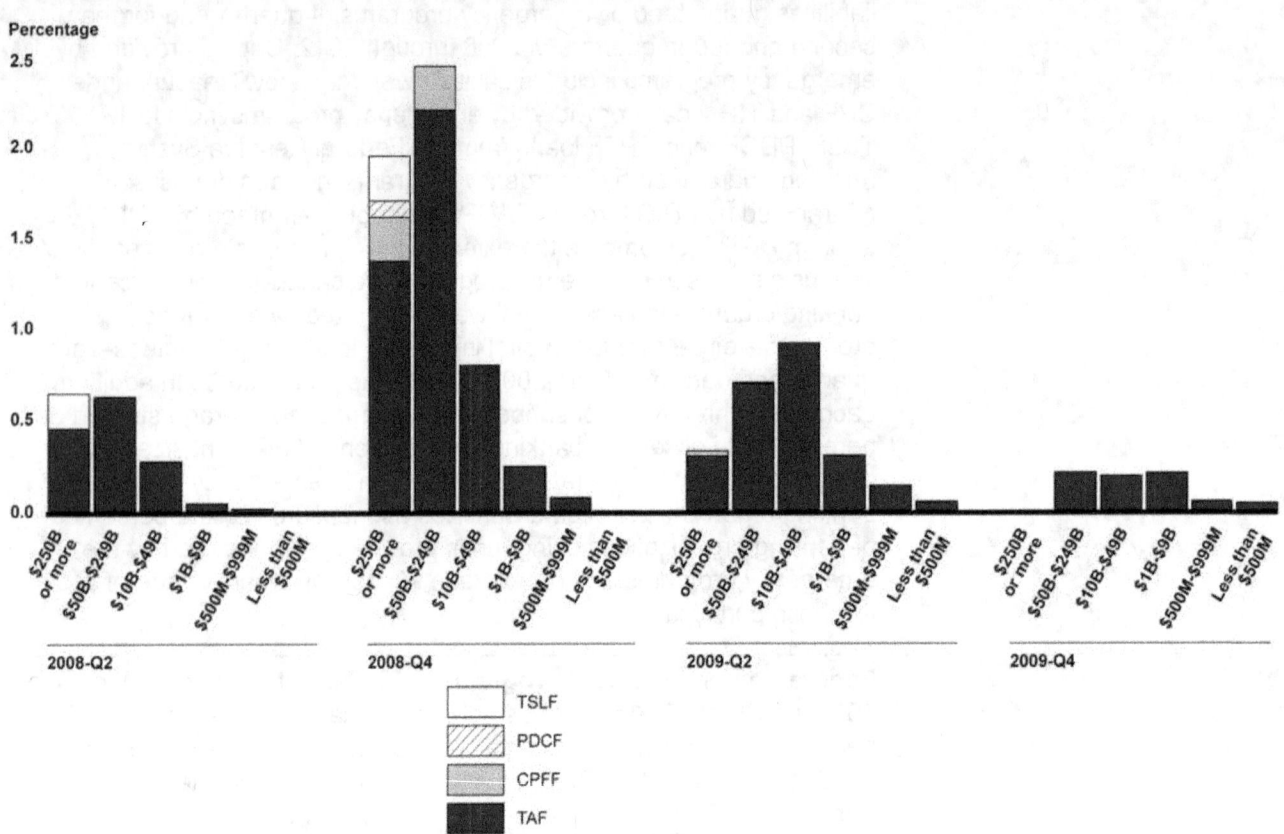

Source: GAO analysis of data from the Bureau of Economic Analysis, FDIC, the Federal Reserve Board, the Federal Reserve Bank of Chicago, SNL Financial, and Treasury.

Note: Banking organizations include consolidated top-tier U.S. bank holding companies and standalone depository institutions. Assets for bank holding companies are consolidated assets for the top-tier bank holding company, which include the assets of consolidated subsidiaries. Assets for standalone depository institutions are consolidated assets for the institution. We exclude banking organizations for which we could not reliably calculate consolidated assets. Banking organizations are divided into groups each quarter using consolidated assets that were first adjusted for inflation and measured in fourth quarter 2012 dollars. Size groups include banking organizations with assets equal to the lower bound but do not include banking organizations with assets equal to the upper bound. For example, banking organizations with $50 billion in assets would be in the "$50-250 billion" group, not the "$10-50 billion" group.

Through mid-2009, the larger banking organizations participated in the four Federal Reserve System programs we analyzed at higher rates than smaller banking organizations (see Panel A of table 4). However, by the end of 2009, banking organizations with $250 billion or more in assets had completely exited all of these programs, but of the remaining institutions, larger banking organizations continued to participate at higher rates than smaller banking organizations. These programs all closed in the first quarter of 2010.[2]

Table 4: Participation Rates and Average Loan Amounts Outstanding as a Percent of Assets at Quarter-End for Participating Banking Organizations for CPFF, PDCF, TAF, and TSLF, June 30, 2008 through December 31, 2009

A. Percent of banking organizations participating in CPFF, PDCF, TAF, or TSLF (%)

Quarter	Assets <$500M	Assets ≥$500M, <$1B	Assets ≥$1B, <$10B	Assets ≥$10B, <$50B	Assets ≥$50B, <$250B	Assets ≥$250B
2008q2	0.03	0.58	2.24	11.86	30.00	75.00
2008q4	0.19	1.78	6.04	26.23	60.00	75.00
2009q2	0.83	3.25	8.48	25.00	38.89	44.44
2009q4	0.66	1.91	5.56	7.02	10.53	0

B. Average CPFF, PDCF, TAF, and TSLF loans outstanding as a percent of assets for participating banking organizations (%)

Quarter	Assets <$500M	Assets ≥$500M, <$1B	Assets ≥$1B, <$10B	Assets ≥$10B, <$50B	Assets ≥$50B, <$250B	Assets ≥$250B
2008q2	8.46	4.30	2.41	2.39	2.11	0.87
2008q4	5.99	4.76	4.27	3.08	4.09	2.61
2009q2	7.56	4.60	3.69	3.70	1.83	0.76
2009q4	7.94	3.31	3.91	2.86	2.09	N/A

Source: GAO analysis of data from BEA, FDIC, the Federal Reserve Board, the Federal Reserve Bank of Chicago, SNL Financial, and Treasury.

Note: Banking organizations include consolidated top-tier U.S. bank holding companies and standalone depository institutions. Assets for bank holding companies are consolidated assets for the top-tier bank holding company, which include the assets of consolidated subsidiaries. Assets for standalone depository institutions are consolidated assets for the institution. We exclude banking organizations for which we could not reliably calculate consolidated assets. Banking organizations are divided into groups each quarter using consolidated assets that were first adjusted for inflation and measured in fourth quarter 2012 dollars. The participation rate is the percentage of banking organizations with CPFF, PDCF, TAF, or TSLF loans outstanding at quarter-end.

Among banking organizations that participated in at least one of the four Federal Reserve programs, average combined CPFF, PDCF, TAF, and TSLF loans outstanding as a percentage of assets were generally larger for smaller participants (see Panel B of table 4). As of the end of 2008, among participating banking organizations, combined CPFF, PDCF, TAF, and TSLF loans outstanding ranged from about 2.6 percent of assets on average for participants with $250 billion or more in assets to about 6.0 percent of assets on average for participants with less than $500 million

[2]The final TAF auction was held in March 2010. However, credit extended under that auction did not mature until April 2010.

in assets. As of the end of 2009, combined CPFF, PDCF, TAF, and TSLF loans outstanding ranged from about 2.1 percent of assets for participants with at least $50 billion but less than $250 billion in assets to about 7.9 percent of assets for banking organizations with less than $500 million in assets, while banking organizations with $250 billion or more in assets were no longer participating in these programs.

Treasury capital investments. Treasury began making equity investments in banking organizations through CPP in October 2008 and it established TIP in December 2008. As of the end of 2008, CPP investment amounts outstanding ranged from about 0.01 percent of assets on average for banking organizations with less than $500 million in assets to about 1.9 percent of assets on average for banking organizations with at least $50 billion but less than $250 billion in assets (see fig. 4). CPP and TIP investment amounts outstanding for banking organizations with $250 billion or more were about 1.6 percent of assets on average.[3] As of mid-2010, banking organizations with $250 billion or more in assets had repaid Treasury and exited CPP and TIP. At the same time, CPP investment amounts had fallen to less than 1 percent of assets on average for banking organizations in all smaller size groups. As of the end of 2012, banking organizations with at least $50 billion but less than $250 billion in assets had repaid Treasury and exited CPP, and CPP investment amounts had fallen to less than 0.25 percent of assets on average for banking organizations in all smaller size groups.[4]

---

[3]Treasury made TIP investments in two banking organizations, Bank of America Corporation and Citigroup, Inc., both of which are in the group of banking organizations with $250 billion or more in assets in every quarter.

[4]Some small banks repaid their CPP investments with funds from Treasury's Small Business Lending Fund (SBLF). As a result, their liability to Treasury remained following their repayment of CPP funds. SBLF is a capital support program that encourages small and midsize banks and community development loan funds to lend to small businesses.

Figure 4: Average CPP and TIP Investment Amounts Outstanding as a Percentage of Assets at Quarter-End for All Banking Organizations by Size, December 31, 2008 through December 31, 2012.

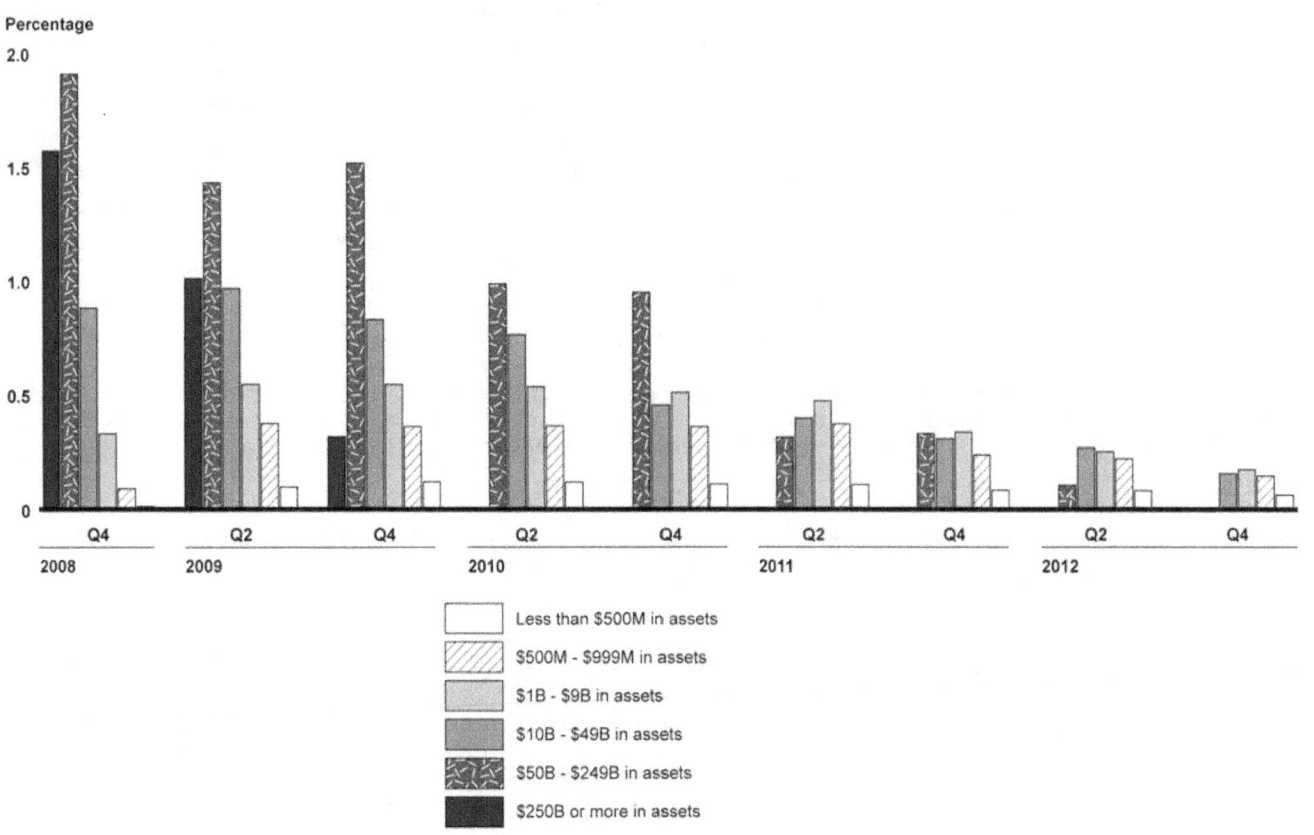

Source: GAO analysis of data from BEA, FDIC, the Federal Reserve Board, the Federal Reserve Bank of Chicago, SNL Financial, and Treasury.

Note: Banking organizations include consolidated top-tier U.S. bank holding companies and standalone depository institutions. Assets for bank holding companies are consolidated assets for the top-tier bank holding company, which include the assets of consolidated subsidiaries. Assets for standalone depository institutions are consolidated assets for the institution. We exclude banking organizations for which we could not reliably calculate consolidated assets. Banking organizations are divided into groups each quarter using consolidated assets that were first adjusted for inflation and measured in fourth quarter 2012 dollars. Size groups include banking organizations with assets equal to the lower bound but do not include banking organizations with assets equal to the upper bound. For example, banking organizations with $50 billion in assets would be in the "$50-250 billion" group, not the "$10-50 billion" group.

At the end of 2008, participation rates in CPP and TIP were higher for larger banking organizations and ranged from about 0.5 percent for banking organizations with less than $500 million in assets to about 87.5 percent for banking organizations with $250 billion or more in assets (see Panel A of Table 5). As of the end of 2010, all banking organizations with

$250 billion or more in assets had repaid Treasury and were no longer participating in CPP or TIP. For banking organizations that continued to participate in CPP, participation rates ranged from about 4.8 percent for banking organizations with less than $500 million in assets to 35 percent for banking organizations with at least $50 billion but less than $250 billion in assets. As of the end of 2012, all banking organizations with $50 billion or more had exited CPP and TIP. For banking organizations that continued to participate in CPP, participation rates ranged from about 2.4 percent for banking organizations with less than $500 million in assets to about 6.5 percent for banking organizations with $1-10 billion in assets (see Panel A of table 5). For participating banking organizations of all sizes, average CPP and TIP amounts outstanding were 2 to 3 percent of assets in most quarters (see Panel B of table 5).

Table 5: Participation Rates and Average Investment Amounts Outstanding as a Percentage of Assets at Quarter-End for Participating Banking Organizations for CPP and TIP, December 31, 2008 to December 31, 2012

A. Percent of banking organizations participating in CPP or TIP at quarter-end (%)

Quarter	Assets <$500M	Assets ≥$500M, <$1B	Assets ≥$1B, <$10B	Assets ≥$10B, <$50B	Assets ≥$50B, <$250B	Assets ≥$250B
2008q4	0.49	4.30	14.65	37.70	80.00	87.50
2009q2	4.57	17.46	25.81	41.67	50.00	44.44
2009q4	5.20	16.89	25.93	36.84	52.63	11.11
2010q2	5.22	17.14	25.38	33.96	35.00	0.00
2010q4	4.75	16.98	23.46	18.87	35.00	0.00
2011q2	4.72	17.24	21.68	16.67	15.79	0.00
2011q4	3.42	10.03	14.59	12.96	16.67	0.00
2012q2	3.32	9.18	10.47	10.91	11.76	0.00
2012q4	2.36	5.68	6.53	5.45	0.00	0.00

B. Average CPP and TIP investment amounts outstanding as a percent of assets at quarter-end for participating banking organizations (%)

Quarter	Assets <$500M	Assets ≥$500M, <$1B	Assets ≥$1B, <$10B	Assets ≥$10B, <$50B	Assets ≥$50B, <$250B	Assets ≥$250B
2008q4	2.25	2.08	2.22	2.33	2.38	1.79
2009q2	2.14	2.12	2.10	2.31	2.86	2.27
2009q4	2.32	2.11	2.09	2.25	2.88	2.81
2010q2	2.28	2.10	2.10	2.24	2.81	N/A
2010q4	2.32	2.10	2.16	2.39	2.71	N/A
2011q2	2.30	2.14	2.16	2.36	1.96	N/A

2011q4	2.42	2.35	2.28	2.34	1.96	N/A
2012q2	2.47	2.38	2.38	2.44	0.89	N/A
2012q4	2.65	2.56	2.66	2.86	N/A	N/A

Source: GAO analysis of data from BEA, FDIC, the Federal Reserve Board, the Federal Reserve Bank of Chicago, and Treasury.

Note: Banking organizations include consolidated top-tier U.S. bank holding companies and standalone depository institutions. Assets for bank holding companies are consolidated assets for the top-tier bank holding company, which include the assets of consolidated subsidiaries. Assets for standalone depository institutions are consolidated assets for the institution. We exclude banking organizations for which we could not reliably calculate consolidated assets. Banking organizations are divided into groups each quarter using consolidated assets that were first adjusted for inflation and measured in fourth quarter 2012 dollars. The participation rate is the percentage of banking organizations with CPP or TIP amounts outstanding at quarter-end.

FDIC's TLGP. FDIC implemented DGP and TAGP, the two components of TLGP, in October 2008. As of the end of 2008, average DGP-guaranteed debt and TAGP-guaranteed deposit amounts outstanding altogether as a percentage of assets were higher for larger banking organizations than smaller banking organizations and ranged from about 1.5 percent of assets on average for banking organizations with less than $500 million in assets to 7.7 percent of assets on average for banking organizations with $250 billion or more in assets (see fig. 5). By the end of 2010, differences in utilization of DGP and TAGP across banking organizations of different sizes had diminished somewhat, with DGP-guaranteed debt and TAGP-guaranteed deposit amounts outstanding altogether ranging from 1.4 percent for banking organizations with $250 billion or more in assets to about 3.2 percent for banking organizations with at least $1 billion but less than $10 billion in assets. TAGP expired on December 31, 2010, and by the end of 2011, DGP-guaranteed debt amounts outstanding were less than 1 percent of assets on average for banking organizations of all sizes. DGP expired on December 31, 2012, so none of the assets of any banking organization were funded using DGP-guaranteed debt after that date.

Figure 5: Average DGP-Guaranteed Debt and TAGP-Guaranteed Deposits Outstanding as a Percentage of Assets at Quarter-End for All Banking Organizations by Size, December 31, 2008, through December 31, 2012

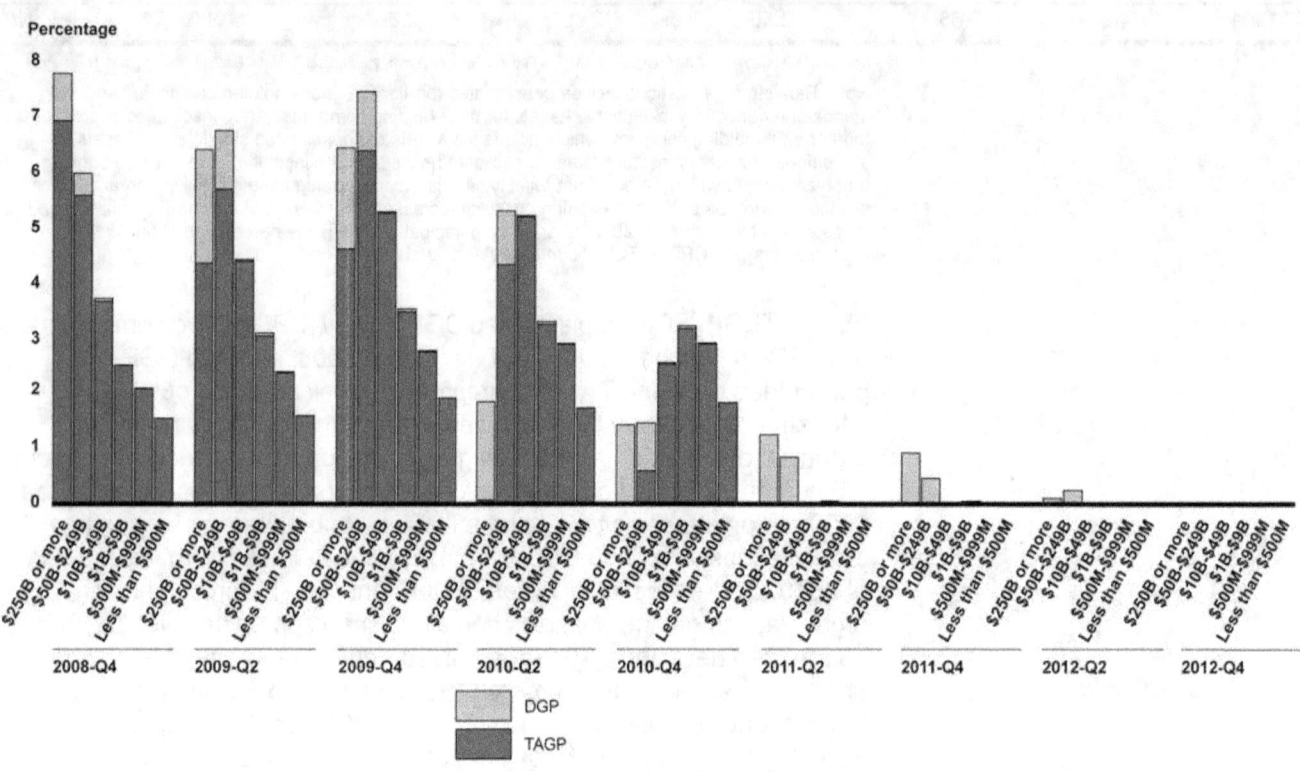

Source: GAO analysis of data from the Bureau of Economic Analysis, FDIC, the Federal Reserve Board, the Federal Reserve Bank of Chicago, SNL Financial, and Treasury.

Note: Banking organizations include consolidated top-tier U.S. bank holding companies and standalone depository institutions. Assets for bank holding companies are consolidated assets for the top-tier bank holding company, which include the assets of consolidated subsidiaries. Assets for standalone depository institutions are consolidated assets for the institution. We exclude banking organizations for which we could not reliably calculate consolidated assets. Banking organizations are divided into groups each quarter using consolidated assets that were first adjusted for inflation and measured in fourth quarter 2012 dollars. Size groups include banking organizations with assets equal to the lower bound but do not include banking organizations with assets equal to the upper bound. For example, banking organizations with $50 billion in assets would be in the "$50-250 billion" group, not the "$10-50 billion" group.

In general, 50 percent or more of the banking organizations in every size group were using either DGP-guaranteed debt or TAGP-guaranteed deposits (or both) as funding through the end of 2010 (see Panel A of table 6). At the end of 2008, participation rates ranged from about 66.3 percent for banking organizations with less than $500 million in assets to about 92.9 percent for banking organizations with at least $1 billion but less than $10 billion in assets. At the end of 2010, participation rates ranged from about 50 percent for banking organizations with at least $50 billion but less than $250 billion in assets to 100 percent for banking organizations with $250 billion or more in assets. Participation rates for banking organizations with less than $50 billion in assets fell after TAGP expired on December 31, 2010, and in mid-2011 ranged from about 0.04 percent for banking organizations with less than $500 million in assets to about 3.1 percent for banking organizations with at least $1 billion but less than $10 billion in assets. Participation rates were about 42.1 percent and 100 percent for banking organizations with at least $50 billion but less than $250 billion in assets and with $250 billion or more in assets, respectively, at that time. By mid-2012, only banking organizations with $50 billion or more were participating in DGP, which then expired at the end of 2012.

Table 6: Participation Rates in DGP and TAGP and Average DGP-Guaranteed Debt and TAGP-Guaranteed Deposits Outstanding as a Percentage of Assets at Quarter-End for Participating Banking Organizations, December 31, 2008, through December 31, 2012

A. Percent of banking organizations participating in DGP, TAGP, or both at quarter-end (%).

Quarter	Assets <$500M	Assets ≥$500M, <$1B	Assets ≥$1B, <$10B	Assets ≥$10B, <$50B	Assets ≥$50B, <$250B	Assets ≥$250B
2008q4	66.27	84.87	92.86	86.89	86.67	87.50
2009q2	66.98	89.79	93.14	88.33	88.89	100.00
2009q4	70.46	90.60	93.89	87.72	89.47	100.00
2010q2	66.56	86.74	87.12	77.36	85.00	100.00
2010q4	65.33	81.48	80.77	45.28	50.00	100.00
2011q2	0.04	0.78	3.13	1.85	42.11	100.00
2011q4	0.04	0.64	2.92	1.85	33.33	100.00
2012q2	0.00	0.00	0.00	0.00	5.88	27.27
2012q4	0.00	0.00	0.00	0.00	0.00	20.00

B. Average DGP-guaranteed debt and TAGP-guaranteed deposit amounts outstanding as a percent of assets for participating banking organizations at quarter end (%).

Quarter	Assets <$500M	Assets ≥$500M, <$1B	Assets ≥$1B, <$10B	Assets ≥$10B, <$50B	Assets ≥$50B, <$250B	Assets ≥$250B
2008q4	2.30	2.42	2.66	4.22	6.82	8.81
2009q2	2.34	2.62	3.27	4.94	7.51	6.34
2009q4	2.67	3.01	3.71	5.96	8.25	6.37
2010q2	2.55	3.29	3.73	6.67	6.16	1.81
2010q4	2.75	3.51	3.93	5.56	2.88	1.41
2011q2	1.75	2.12	1.61	1.48	1.99	1.23

GAO-14-18 Government Support for Bank Holding Companies

2011q4	1.72	1.72	1.58	0.21	1.37	0.91
2012q2	N/A	N/A	N/A	N/A	4.14	0.38
2012q4	N/A	N/A	N/A	N/A	N/A	<0.01

Source: GAO analysis of data from BEA, FDIC, the Federal Reserve Board, the Federal Reserve Bank of Chicago, and Treasury.

Note: Banking organizations include consolidated top-tier U.S. bank holding companies and standalone depository institutions. Assets for bank holding companies are consolidated assets for the top-tier bank holding company, which include the assets of consolidated subsidiaries. Assets for standalone depository institutions are consolidated assets for the institution. We exclude banking organizations for which we could not reliably calculate consolidated assets. Banking organizations are divided into groups each quarter using consolidated assets that were first adjusted for inflation and measured in fourth quarter 2012 dollars. The participation rate is the percentage of banking organizations with positive amounts of TAGP-guaranteed deposits or DGP-guaranteed debt outstanding at quarter-end.

At the end of 2008, average DGP-guaranteed debt and TAGP-guaranteed deposit amounts outstanding were higher as a percentage of assets for larger participants than for smaller participants and ranged from about 2.3 percent for participants with less than $500 million in assets to about 8.8 percent for participants with $250 billion or more in assets (see Panel B of table 6). At the end of 2010, average DGP-guaranteed debt and TAGP-guaranteed deposit amounts outstanding as a percentage of assets had fallen for banking organizations with $50 billion or more in assets but not for smaller banking organizations. At that time, DGP-guaranteed debt and TAGP-guaranteed deposit amounts outstanding ranged from about 1.4 percent of assets on average for participants with $250 billion or more in assets to about 5.6 percent of assets on average for participants with $10-50 billion in assets. TAGP expired on December 31, 2010, and as of the end of 2011, DGP-guaranteed debt amounts outstanding were less than 2 percent of assets on average for banking organizations of all sizes. DGP expired on December 31, 2012.

Lastly, our analysis found that the six largest bank holding companies as of December 31, 2012—all with consolidated assets greater than $500 billion—used the emergency programs to varying degrees but had exited most by the end of 2009. Table 7 shows the percentage of consolidated assets funded by DGP-guaranteed debt, TAGP-guaranteed deposits, TAF loans, CPFF loans, PDCF loans, TSLF loans, and CPP and TIP equity investments for the largest bank holding companies at year-end from 2008 to 2012. For comparison purposes we also show the average percent of assets funded by the same programs for the six banking organization size groups over the same period.

Table 7. Average outstanding amounts of equity provided, loans provided, and liabilities guaranteed by emergency programs for select bank holding companies and for banking organizations by size at year end, 2008-2012.

	DGP-guaranteed debt outstanding	TAGP-guaranteed deposits outstanding	TAF loans outstanding	CPFF loans outstanding	PDCF loans outstanding	Market value of TSLF loans outstanding	CPP and TIP investment amounts outstanding
Select banking organizations as of December 31, 2008:							
Bank of America Corporation							
% of assets	2.44	5.53	2.47	0.82	0	0	0.82
$ billions	44.55	100.69	45.00	14.93	0	0	15.00
Citigroup, Inc.							
% of assets	1.64	2.50	0.77	0.64	0.71	1.87	2.32
$ billions	31.87	48.41	15.00	12.39	13.80	36.19	45.00
Goldman Sachs Group, Inc.[a]							
% of assets	—	—	—	—	—	—	—
$ billions	—	—	—	—	—	—	—
JPMorgan Chase & Co.							
% of assets	0.96	6.24	1.38	0	0	0.11	1.15
$ billions	20.93	135.73	30.00	0	0	2.46	25.00
Morgan Stanley[a]							
% of assets	—	—	—	—	—	—	—
$ billions	—	—	—	—	—	—	—
Wells Fargo & Company							
% of assets	0.46	4.85	5.54	0	0	0	1.91
$ billions	6.08	63.48	72.50	0	0	0	25.00
Average for banking organizations by size as of December 31, 2008:							
Assets ≥ $250 billion							
% of assets	0.86	6.85	1.38	0.24	0.09	0.25	1.57
$ billions	13.42	54.84	20.68	3.68	1.72	4.83	15.90
Assets $50-250 billion							
% of assets	0.40	5.52	2.21	0.24	0	0	1.91
$ billions	0.59	6.63	2.55	0.40	0	0	2.09
Assets $10-50 billion							
% of assets	0.05	3.61	0.81	0	0	0	0.88
$ billions	0.01	0.59	0.18	0	0	0	0.15
Assets $1-10 billion							
% of assets	<0.01	2.47	0.26	0	0	0	0.32
$ billions	<0.01	0.06	0.01	0	0	0	0.01

	DGP-guaranteed debt outstanding	TAGP-guaranteed deposits outstanding	TAF loans outstanding	CPFF loans outstanding	PDCF loans outstanding	Market value of TSLF loans outstanding	CPP and TIP investment amounts outstanding
Assets $500 million to $1 billion							
% of assets	0.01	2.04	0.08	0	0	0	0.09
$ billions	<0.01	0.01	<0.01	0	0	0	<0.01
Assets < $500 million							
% of assets	<0.01	1.52	0.01	0	0	0	0.01
$ billions	<0.01	<0.01	<0.01	0	0	0	<0.01
Select banking organizations as of December 31, 2009:							
Bank of America Corporation							
% of assets	1.99	7.22	0	0	0	0	0
$ billions	44.31	161.02	0	0	0	0	0
Citigroup, Inc.							
% of assets	3.52	2.71	0	0	0	0	0
$ billions	65.59	50.56	0	0	0	0	0
Goldman Sachs Group, Inc.							
% of assets	2.42	0.26	0	0	0	0	0
$ billions	20.57	2.19	0	0	0	0	0
JPMorgan Chase & Co.							
% of assets	1.99	5.53	0	0	0	0	0
$ billions	40.48	112.29	0	0	0	0	0
Morgan Stanley							
% of assets	3.08	1.01	0	0	0	0	0
$ billions	23.77	7.76	0	0	0	0	0
Wells Fargo & Company							
% of assets	0.77	7.38	0	0	0	0	0
$ billions	9.52	91.82	0	0	0	0	0
Average for banking organizations by size as of December 31, 2009:							
Assets ≥ $250 billion							
% of assets	1.81	4.56	0	0	0	0	0.31
$ billions	23.48	52.49	0	0	0	0	0.84
Assets $50-250 billion							
% of assets	1.07	6.32	0.22	0	0	0	1.52
$ billions	1.47	7.12	0.37	0	0	0	1.29
Assets $10-50 billion							
% of assets	0.03	5.20	0.20	0	0	0	0.83

	DGP-guaranteed debt outstanding	TAGP-guaranteed deposits outstanding	TAF loans outstanding	CPFF loans outstanding	PDCF loans outstanding	Market value of TSLF loans outstanding	CPP and TIP investment amounts outstanding
$ billions	0.01	0.80	0.04	0	0	0	0.14
Assets $1-10 billion							
% of assets	0.05	3.43	0.22	0	0	0	0.54
$ billions	<0.01	0.08	0.01	0	0	0	0.01
Assets $500 million-1 billion							
% of assets	0.02	2.71	0.06	0	0	0	0.36
$ billions	<0.01	0.02	<0.01	0	0	0	<0.01
Assets <$500 million							
% of assets	<0.01	1.88	0.05	0	0	0	0.12
$ billions	<0.01	<0.01	<0.01	0	0	0	<0.01
Select banking organizations as of December 31, 2010:							
Bank of America Corporation							
% of assets	1.21	0	0	0	0	0	0
$ billions	27.45	0	0	0	0	0	0
Citigroup, Inc.							
% of assets	3.04	0	0	0	0	0	0
$ billions	58.25	0	0	0	0	0	0
Goldman Sachs Group, Inc.							
% of assets	2.07	0	0	0	0	0	0
$ billions	18.84	0	0	0	0	0	0
JPMorgan Chase & Co.							
% of assets	1.71	0	0	0	0	0	0
$ billions	36.13	0	0	0	0	0	0
Morgan Stanley							
% of assets	2.63	0	0	0	0	0	0
$ billions	21.27	0	0	0	0	0	0
Wells Fargo & Company							
% of assets	0.76	0	0	0	0	0	0
$ billions	9.50	0	0	0	0	0	0
Average for banking organizations by size as of December 31, 2010:							
Assets ≥ $250 billion							
% of assets	1.41	0	0	0	0	0	0
$ billions	17.90	0	0	0	0	0	0

	DGP-guaranteed debt outstanding	TAGP-guaranteed deposits outstanding	TAF loans outstanding	CPFF loans outstanding	PDCF loans outstanding	Market value of TSLF loans outstanding	CPP and TIP investment amounts outstanding
Assets $50-250 billion							
% of assets	0.85	0.59	0	0	0	0	0.95
$ billions	1.19	0.30	0	0	0	0	0.92
Assets $10-50 billion							
% of assets	0.03	2.49	0	0	0	0	0.45
$ billions	0.01	0.42	0	0	0	0	0.08
Assets $1-10 billion							
% of assets	0.05	3.12	0	0	0	0	0.51
$ billions	<0.01	0.08	0	0	0	0	0.01
Assets $500 million-1 billion							
% of assets	0.02	2.84	0	0	0	0	0.36
$ billions	<0.01	0.02	0	0	0	0	<0.01
Assets <$500 million							
% of assets	<0.01	1.80	0	0	0	0	0.11
$ billions	<0.01	<0.01	0	0	0	0	<0.01
Select banking organizations as of December 31, 2011:							
Bank of America Corporation							
% of assets	1.12	0	0	0	0	0	0
$ billions	23.85	0	0	0	0	0	0
Citigroup, Inc.							
% of assets	2.03	0	0	0	0	0	0
$ billions	38.00	0	0	0	0	0	0
Goldman Sachs Group, Inc.							
% of assets	0.92	0	0	0	0	0	0
$ billions	8.50	0	0	0	0	0	0
JPMorgan Chase & Co.							
% of assets	0.89	0	0	0	0	0	0
$ billions	20.18	0	0	0	0	0	0
Morgan Stanley							
% of assets	1.75	0	0	0	0	0	0
$ billions	13.09	0	0	0	0	0	0
Wells Fargo & Company							
% of assets	0.27	0	0	0	0	0	0
$ billions	3.50	0	0	0	0	0	0

	DGP-guaranteed debt outstanding	TAGP-guaranteed deposits outstanding	TAF loans outstanding	CPFF loans outstanding	PDCF loans outstanding	Market value of TSLF loans outstanding	CPP and TIP investment amounts outstanding
Average for banking organizations by size as of December 31, 2011:							
Assets ≥ $250 billion							
% of assets	0.91	0	0	0	0	0	0
$ billions	11.38	0	0	0	0	0	0
Assets $50-250 billion							
% of assets	0.46	0	0	0	0	0	0.33
$ billions	0.65	0	0	0	0	0	0.29
Assets $10-50 billion							
% of assets	<0.01	0	0	0	0	0	0.30
$ billions	<0.01	0	0	0	0	0	0.06
Assets $1-10 billion							
% of assets	0.05	0	0	0	0	0	0.33
$ billions	<0.01	0	0	0	0	0	0.01
Assets $500 million-1 billion							
% of assets	0.01	0	0	0	0	0	0.24
$ billions	<0.01	0	0	0	0	0	<0.01
Assets <$500 million							
% of assets	<0.01	0	0	0	0	0	0.08
$ billions	<0.01	0	0	0	0	0	<0.01
Select banking organizations as of December 31, 2012:							
Bank of America Corporation							
% of assets	0	0	0	0	0	0	0
$ billions	0	0	0	0	0	0	0
Citigroup, Inc.							
% of assets	<0.01	0	0	0	0	0	0
$ billions	<0.01	0	0	0	0	0	0
Goldman Sachs Group, Inc.							
% of assets	0	0	0	0	0	0	0
$ billions	0	0	0	0	0	0	0
JPMorgan Chase & Co.							
% of assets	0	0	0	0	0	0	0
$ billions	0	0	0	0	0	0	0
Morgan Stanley							
% of assets	0	0	0	0	0	0	0

	DGP-guaranteed debt outstanding	TAGP-guaranteed deposits outstanding	TAF loans outstanding	CPFF loans outstanding	PDCF loans outstanding	Market value of TSLF loans outstanding	CPP and TIP investment amounts outstanding
$ billions	0	0	0	0	0	0	0
Wells Fargo & Company							
% of assets	<0.01	0	0	0	0	0	0
$ billions	<0.01	0	0	0	0	0	0
Average for banking organizations by size as of December 31, 2012:							
Assets ≥ $250 billion							
% of assets	<0.01	0	0	0	0	0	0
$ billions	<0.01	0	0	0	0	0	0
Assets $50-250 billion							
% of assets	0	0	0	0	0	0	0
$ billions	0	0	0	0	0	0	0
Assets $10-50 billion							
% of assets	0	0	0	0	0	0	0.16
$ billions	0	0	0	0	0	0	0.04
Assets $1-10 billion							
% of assets	0	0	0	0	0	0	0.17
$ billions	0	0	0	0	0	0	<0.01
Assets $500 million-1 billion							
% of assets	0	0	0	0	0	0	0.15
$ billions	0	0	0	0	0	0	<0.01
Assets <$500 million							
% of assets	0	0	0	0	0	0	0.06
$ billions	0	0	0	0	0	0	<0.01

Source: GAO analysis of data from BEA, FDIC, the Federal Reserve Board, the Federal Reserve Bank of Chicago, SNL Financial, and Treasury.

Note: Banking organizations include consolidated top-tier U.S. bank holding companies and standalone depository institutions. Assets for bank holding companies are consolidated assets for the top-tier bank holding company, which include the assets of consolidated subsidiaries. Assets for standalone depository institutions are consolidated assets for the institution. We exclude banking organizations for which we could not reliably calculate consolidated assets. Select bank holding companies are those with $500 billion or more in assets as of December 31, 2012. Banking organizations are divided into groups each quarter using consolidated assets that were first adjusted for inflation and measured in fourth quarter 2012 dollars.

[a]Goldman Sachs Group, Inc. and Morgan Stanley became bank holding companies in September 2008 but did not file form FR Y-9C, the source of our data on consolidated assets, for the fourth quarter of 2008.

Appendix V: Comments from the Board of Governors of the Federal Reserve System

BOARD OF GOVERNORS
OF THE
FEDERAL RESERVE SYSTEM
WASHINGTON, D. C. 20551

SCOTT G. ALVAREZ
GENERAL COUNSEL

October 17, 2013

Lawrance L. Evans, Jr.
Director, Financial Markets
   And Community Investment
Government Accountability Office
441 G Street, N.W.
Washington, D.C. 20548

Dear Mr. Evans:

Thank you for the opportunity to comment on your draft report numbered GAO-14-18. As the draft report notes, "During the financial crisis, the Federal Reserve System, Treasury and the FDIC introduced new programs with broad-based eligibility to provide general funding support to the financial sector and to stabilize the financial system."[1] GAO further concludes that "collectively these interventions helped to improve financial stability by enhancing confidence in financial institutions and the financial system overall. Bank holding companies and their subsidiaries, in addition to the financial sector and the economy as a whole, benefited from improved stability."[2] Clearly, the assistance discussed in this report was broad based and not exclusive to bank holding companies.

As GAO knows, all of the Federal Reserve and FDIC assistance was fully repaid with interest. It would be helpful, perhaps in a future report, to add to the discussion of benefits to bank holding companies some analysis about the offsetting costs paid by bank holding companies and other financial institutions assisted through the emergency programs.

The draft report includes one recommendation to the Federal Reserve Board: that the Chairman take steps to draft and finalize policies and procedures governing the use of emergency lending programs under Section 13(3) of the Federal Reserve Act. We accept this recommendation and are already working in this direction. The Chairman noted in testimony before Congress on July 17, 2013, that the Board has made progress on a rule and is hopeful that a final product will be ready relatively soon, perhaps by the end of the year. In the

---

[1] U.S. GOV'T ACCOUNTABILITY OFFICE, GOVERNMENT SUPPORT FOR BANK HOLDING COMPANIES, STATUTORY CHANGES TO LIMIT FUTURE SUPPORT ARE NOT FULLY IMPLEMENTED at 11(Draft report 2013).
[2] Id. at 16.

2.

meantime, as the Chairman noted in his testimony, the law is clear about what the Board of
Governors can and cannot do. Your draft report also references the fact that the Board could,
today, take decisive action, consistent with the new 13(3) language, in the event of another
financial crisis. [3] In accordance with the recommendation in the draft report and the Chairman's
intentions, the Board will continue to take steps to finalize the policies and procedures associated
with the new 13(3) authority.

Thank you again for providing us an opportunity to comment on your draft report.

Sincerely,

Scott G. Alvarez

---

[3] Id. at 45.

Appendix VI: Comments from the Department of the Treasury

DEPARTMENT OF THE TREASURY
WASHINGTON, D C

UNDER SECRETARY

November 4, 2013

Lawrance L. Evans, Jr.
Director
Financial Markets and Community Investment
Government Accountability Office
441 G. Street, NW
Washington, DC 20548

Dear Mr. Evans:

I am writing regarding the Government Accountability Office's (GAO) draft report GAO-14-18 (the Draft Report) on government support for bank holding companies during the 2007-2009 financial crisis.

We appreciate the GAO's work in this area. The report found that the federal government's provision of funding support during the financial crisis to bank holding companies and their bank and nonbank financial subsidiaries helped to improve U.S. financial stability by enhancing confidence in financial institutions and the financial system overall. The emergency programs introduced during the crisis were necessary to prevent a collapse of the financial system. In addition to averting a severe crisis, these actions created economic benefits not only for individual firms, large and small, but also for the financial system and the broader economy. As the GAO has previously noted, taxpayers have already recovered more from Treasury's Troubled Asset Relief Program than was disbursed, including Treasury's positive returns from its investment in American International Group, Inc.

The emergency programs implemented during the crisis were not meant to be permanent and the Draft Report recognizes this. We appreciate the GAO's analysis and conclusion that the Dodd-Frank Wall Street Reform and Consumer Protection Act (Dodd-Frank) modifies and curtails federal authorities to provide support to financial firms and strengthens regulatory oversight of the largest firms. The particular reforms cited in the Draft Report, among others in Dodd-Frank and under international agreements, were put in place to reduce the risk to the financial system that any one firm can pose and to give regulators important tools that they lacked during the financial crisis to resolve a failing firm while limiting the fallout to the rest of the financial system and economy. These reforms are consistent with our commitment to ending "too big to fail," and also serve to level the playing field between the largest and smaller firms.

Thank you again for the opportunity to review the Draft Report. We look forward to continuing to work with you and your team as we move forward.

Sincerely,

Mary J. Miller

Appendix VII: GAO Contact and Staff Acknowledgments

GAO Contact	Lawrance L. Evans, Jr., (202) 512-4802, or EvansL@gao.gov
Staff Acknowledgments	In addition to the contact named above, Karen Tremba (Assistant Director), Jordan Anderson, Bethany M. Benitez, Stephanie Cheng, John Fisher, Michael Hoffman, Risto Laboski, Courtney LaFountain, Jon Menaster, Marc Molino, Robert Rieke, and Jennifer Schwartz made key contributions to this report.

GAO's Mission	The Government Accountability Office, the audit, evaluation, and investigative arm of Congress, exists to support Congress in meeting its constitutional responsibilities and to help improve the performance and accountability of the federal government for the American people. GAO examines the use of public funds; evaluates federal programs and policies; and provides analyses, recommendations, and other assistance to help Congress make informed oversight, policy, and funding decisions. GAO's commitment to good government is reflected in its core values of accountability, integrity, and reliability.
Obtaining Copies of GAO Reports and Testimony	The fastest and easiest way to obtain copies of GAO documents at no cost is through GAO's website (http://www.gao.gov). Each weekday afternoon, GAO posts on its website newly released reports, testimony, and correspondence. To have GAO e-mail you a list of newly posted products, go to http://www.gao.gov and select "E-mail Updates."
Order by Phone	The price of each GAO publication reflects GAO's actual cost of production and distribution and depends on the number of pages in the publication and whether the publication is printed in color or black and white. Pricing and ordering information is posted on GAO's website, http://www.gao.gov/ordering.htm. Place orders by calling (202) 512-6000, toll free (866) 801-7077, or TDD (202) 512-2537. Orders may be paid for using American Express, Discover Card, MasterCard, Visa, check, or money order. Call for additional information.
Connect with GAO	Connect with GAO on Facebook, Flickr, Twitter, and YouTube. Subscribe to our RSS Feeds or E-mail Updates. Listen to our Podcasts. Visit GAO on the web at www.gao.gov.
To Report Fraud, Waste, and Abuse in Federal Programs	Contact: Website: http://www.gao.gov/fraudnet/fraudnet.htm E-mail: fraudnet@gao.gov Automated answering system: (800) 424-5454 or (202) 512-7470
Congressional Relations	Katherine Siggerud, Managing Director, siggerudk@gao.gov, (202) 512-4400, U.S. Government Accountability Office, 441 G Street NW, Room 7125, Washington, DC 20548
Public Affairs	Chuck Young, Managing Director, youngc1@gao.gov, (202) 512-4800 U.S. Government Accountability Office, 441 G Street NW, Room 7149 Washington, DC 20548